THE BOOK THAT MAKES YOU RICH

BY: MICHEAL J.RAMSEY

Disclaimer

This book contains performance data. Presentation of this data does not mean that the same or similar results will be achieved in the future. Past performance is no indication of future results, and any claim to the contrary would be unlawful. The data are provided only for illustrative and comparative purposes. A variety of time periods are illustrated. Rather than focus on any one-time period, the reader is encouraged to concentrate and learn from the educational message contained therein.

None of the material presented herein is intended to serve as the basis for any financial, tax, accounting, legal, personal, business or real estate decision. None of the enclosed information constitutes a recommendation or offer to buy or sell any security. Such an offer would be made elsewhere by prospectus, which you should read carefully before investing or sending money.

Contracts regarding real estate, including transfers, must be in writing. Since contracts involve laws of countries, states and municipalities, it is recommended that you seek legal counsel. In my presentation and my writings, I touch upon subjects that could vary in different parts of the United States. I do not vouch for the legality of my opinions, nor is there intent to supply legal advice.

The material herein is accurate to the best of the author's knowledge. However, the author's opinions may change. The reader is encouraged to verify the status of those opinions.

This publication is designed to provide accurate and authoritative information in regard to the subject matter covered. It is sold with the understanding that the publisher is not engaged in rendering legal, accounting, or other professional service. If legal advice or other expert assistance is required, the services of a competent professional person should be sought.

Table Of Contents

Table Of Contents 3
Introduction 4
Online Income 6
   "Infopreneuring" 6
   Opt-In List Marketing 10
   Permission-Based Email Marketing 14
   Affiliate Programs 15
   Niche Marketing 17
   Your Own Web Site Must Act Like a Funnel 19
   Bibliography: 21
Self-Publishing 26
   Three Ways to Write a Book 26
   Getting Your Book Edited 27
   The Next Step 27
   Copyrights and ISBN 28
   Self Published Bestsellers 29
   Other Publications Besides a Book: 30
   Quick Self-Publishing Tips 36
   Glossary of Self Publishing Terms 36
   Bibliography: 37
Network Marketing 47
   Success Factors 47
   Is There a Downside? 48
   What Works 49
   How to Prospect and Approach Inside and Outside Your "Warm" Market and Have Fun Doing It: 49
   REMEMBER! 50
   Advertising 51
   Tips For Getting Started 52
   Bibliography: 54
Direct Mail/Mail Order 61
   List Selection 62
   Before You Start 63
   Checking Your Sales Letter (Copy) 63
   The Advantages of Direct Mail 64
   Using Direct Mail to Create Income 64
   Bibliography: 67
Franchising 71
   The History of Franchising 71
   Types of Franchises 72
   Advantages of Franchise Ownership 73
   Buying a Franchise 74
   Steps to Acquiring a Franchise 75
   Creating Your Own Franchise 79
   Bibliography: 81

Introduction

So, why exactly is the internet such a great place to earn an income? What makes it any better than the "real world"?

The online world is not necessarily a better place to make money, it is different and in many ways a lot easier and a lot less time consuming than making money in the real world.

First off, there is the physical aspect of it. All of the internet world is right in front of your eyes, everything is just a click away, which makes it a lot less time consuming to perform your daily tasks.

Then, there is the cost aspect – it's incredibly cheap to own your own business on the internet! You can literally start earning money on line for as little as $10!

And if you want your own online business, all you need is a hosting account ($10 a month) and a payment processor (free) and you're all ready to go. When comparing that to owning a "real world" business, where rent, employee wages and the sheer amount of work is not only extremely pricy but time consuming as well.

And of course, there is the ability to fully automate your online business without having to hire any employees and have your business work for you 24/7 (the internet is always open) and earn you money while you sleep.

Here is a simple example of the how easy it is to build a passive income stream on the internet when comparing the amount of work it would take you to do the same in the "real world"

To get a passive income of $1,000 a month in the real world, you could by a Condo for $100,000 - $150,000 and rent it out to receive rental income. Do you have $150,000 cash lying around? Probably not.

What you could do online is buy resell rights to an already made information product ($300 would buy you a good one), get online hosting ($10 a month) and start driving traffic to the website. All this can be done in just a few hours, and can easily earn you $30 - $60 a day!

Now you see the difference between the real world and the online world?

The point is: to start making money in the "real world" one usually needs a great amount of time, resources and money. Online, all you need is a few hundred bucks and 1-3 hours a day to invest into your venture.

Ok, I'm sure I've got you a little excited to get started. But there are other great ways for you to make residual income without having your own website, there is also self publishing, Network Marketing, Direct mail etc. which I will also cover in this eBook...

Online Income

Before the internet, information was not always easy to come by. If you needed a recipe, you would most likely have to go to the book store and buy a cook book or go to the library. If you ever wondered how something works, you could only guess or of course go to the library again.

In other words, before the internet information was NOT at our fingertips like it is now.

Have you ever found yourself sitting on the couch, seeing something on TV and wondering "Cool, I want to know more about that" and all you have to do is simply go to your computer and type what ever it is you are looking for into google and all of a sudden you had everything you needed.

With the help of the internet, there has been an information explosion and with this information explosion, six ongoing trends have formed:

"Infopreneuring"

It is not information, however, that we need more of! We are already drowning in information. The problem is not a lack of information or ideas but a lack of information that is packaged properly. Information needs to be categorized into specialized knowledge that the consumer can use quickly. This is the job of an infopreneur – an entrepreneur that sells information.

So, how can you be an infopreneur? Anyone with a good idea and some persistence can do it!! You just need an interesting story or expertise that people want PLUS good marketing skills! Your life story or your life's expertise have market value. You don't even need a unique, new system. It can be old knowledge, repackaged and remarketed in new ways. Look at all the diets out there. There are only 3 variables in the diet game: food, exercise and mental attitude.

The formula is pretty simple:

1. Identify a Core Human Desire/Need
2. Find new technology for solving this Core Desire/Need and/or find a new way to market to this Core Desire/Need

With a winning idea, and many different media to market it, you can then branch into many related support products....bringing in more residual income (see creating a funnel in the last section of this chapter).

There are 3 Essential Skills that you need as an infopreneur:

1. How to research, discover, acquire, and organize your ideas. What do you know that we don't? Or who do you know that knows something that the rest of us need or want to know? You don't have to spend years learning a core expertise. You can find some expert who is under-marketed and take his or her idea to the marketplace. Just remember to organize this information in the communication age style....easy to learn, simple to use,

2. How to express, display, package, communicate yourself. Here are some core packaging skills you will need to develop, rent or acquire:

- Find the best prices for materials
- Designing useful, interesting packaging.
- Creating low cost ways to organize your materials

3. How to sell, distribute, disseminate, promote yourself and your product. Marketing is the essential skill. Here are some core marketing skills which you will have to buy, rent or acquire:

- Writing compelling copy
- Understanding psychology and human nature
- Learning the secrets of direct mail advertising
- Buying the best and cheapest advertising.
- Tracking your results.
- Managing a database.
- Tapping into the Internet

You must have a core expertise that is either a revolutionary new technology or is an old expertise that has a new marketing strategy. As I said earlier, you don't have to be the expert yourself. But you do need to borrow, license, acquire the expertise from someone. You are looking for an expertise that has a large and growing body of interested people who can be easily identified, who have an immediate need/want/problem that they are highly motivated to solve, who have the money to spend and are willing to spend it.

Once you have identified your market and your expertise then, the process of figuring out how to market your information in a way that causes people to want to buy it! Basically, there are no real new or totally unique human needs or wants. They have been the same for thousands of years: sex, money, self-esteem, health, relationships, beauty, greed. Your information should tap into one of these universal wants/needs. The title you select, the words you use to market your information, the benefits your information offers, the way it is packaged will cause consumers to flock to your product. Once you have discovered the right combination of message and media, you

Here is an example of steps to follow to become an infopreneur. Let's say that you are passionate about cooking with hot spices.

1. Brainstorm the most profitable topics

2. Deliver hot and sensual content.

3. Publish quality, in-demand information. You'll be surprised at how quickly a following develops.

4. Monetize... Google AdSense automatically places relevant ads on your site, generating an excellent financial foundation. Refer pre-sold visitors to the affiliate programs of Barnes and Nobles for spicy cookbooks, and other merchants for cookware, food processors, and so forth. In-context textual recommendations from a trusted advisor convert into sales. Similarly, earn income by creating a page about the best spice retailer in each of the 100 largest cities around the world. Get paid via a pay-per-lead model from each. Increase revenues by selling your own e-book of "The World's Hottest, Most Exotic Recipes... Cooking with Fire." Even promote your own "hot 'n spicy" catering

There is no limit to the number of ways to monetize your traffic -- the above are only a few possible examples for the "hot 'n spicy" niche. Nor is there a limit to the number of niches in the small business world...

Robert Allen published a book in 1980 called Nothing Down: How to Buy Real Estate with Little or No Money Down. It took over two years before the money started to flow. But it was worth the wait. Since that time, he has earned millions of dollars in royalties. And every six months he still gets nice royalty checks. That's the power of residual income...it keeps flowing and flowing and flowing.

Here are 8 tips that will help you get started producing audiotapes, books, reports, pamphlets, or any other medium you choose to sell to distribute your information:

1- Produce an information product for an audience that's already waiting to buy it. This will guarantee your greatest chance for success.

2- Clearly identify your target market and direct all your promotional materials towards them. When promoting and marketing your product, first identify the it's purpose. Then find a target market that will benefit from it. Once you've done that, find ways to bring them your message. Speak to them in ways they can relate both to your product and to you. The rapport this builds between you and your prospective buyers will ultimately lead to sales.

3- Always test the market before producing anything. This will save you time and money, if, by chance, you're not on the right track. If test marketing indicates your target market has no interest in the information your product provides, simply redirect your focus, find another topic, and start again with enthusiasm. Or stick with the same topic but find another market that may be interested in what you have to say.

4- Keep your products simple, yet highly informational. Remember the concept is not to compete with Hollywood, but to offer valuable information to specific groups of people who share the same interest.

5- Never stop searching for effective ways to promote your products and reach your target market. Marketing is everything.

6- Create ancillary products such as special reports, audio tapes, and books to complement your initial product

7- Seek out others in your industry who might be willing to joint venture with you on a project.

8- Establish an effective order taking system. Keeping track of your sales, your customers, advertising responses, and your shipping is critical if you plan on being successful.

Opt-In List Marketing

The only things that matter in real estate are location, location and location. The only things that matter for your web site are traffic, traffic and traffic. Just because you launched that spiffy looking new web site or you've created some sharp autoresponders, there's no guarantee that someone will find you. You must drive traffic to your site. More specifically, you need to funnel prospects and clients into your autoresponder or steer people to your web site on an ongoing

One method to acquire email addresses is referred to as the opt-in list. This is where someone has voluntarily given you her/his email address in exchange for some free or low-cost item. Or maybe they responded to an ad you placed somewhere on the Internet. Or maybe that person attended one of your presentations. Maybe, as we'll see in just a bit, that person has come to you as a result of some affiliate program you are a member of. The key is to get the email address.

Over time, as more and more people volunteer their email addresses, you are building a database of names that are of like-minded people. That database is the opt-in list of names of people that have given you permission to stay in touch with them. This will form the basis of what I call permission-based email marketing (see number 2 below).

My opt-in list is composed of people who fit into one of four general categories:

1. Business owners and professionals, or anyone who wants to build or enhance their personal, interpersonal and electronic networking skills.

2. They want to learn how to use those skills to grow their career or business, or to market themselves more creatively and effectively.

3. They want to generate multiple sources of income.

4. They are interested in leveraged or residual income, or they currently make a living via residual income based activities, e.g., insurance salespeople, bankers, real estate investors, web site owners, etc.

Many times, these categories overlap. Marketing 101 dictates that you define your audience before you set out to meet their needs. This is a key reason why there are far more dot-bombs than winning dot-coms: too many sites searching for a market. Each of the following two diagrams contains a step-by-step flow chart of the stages you would go through to acquire email addresses. The first Opt-In List Direct diagram illustrates how you will get leads directly as a result of your advertisement. The second, Two-Step Opt-In List, is basically the same procedure, but it allows you to make some money along the way. These serve as "templates", and you can even use them to get paid simply for the act of acquiring the leads. Won't that be nice!?

By the way, before we review the templates, a word about SPAM. SPAM is unsolicited email that has not been requested by the recipient. Never, never, never, never, never, NEVER SPAM!!!! I cannot emphasize this strongly enough. Always get permission from the recipients of your message before you send the email.

If you send to a list that you bought, obtain written permission from the list vendor as to the permission rights of the list. If the vendor will not provide that permission, don't do business with them. If someone voluntarily opts into your list, ensure that the autoresponder, or whatever other service you're using, provides an audit trail as to where, how and when that request came in. If you are using leads you got from, say a speaking engagement, retain the written record of the request to be added to your list.

And one last piece of CYA (cover your assets) advice. If you get a listing of names and email addresses from an organization, e.g., the membership list of a group for which you made a presentation, make sure you retain the permission letter or email message attached to the list. If someone goes to your information service provider (ISP) and gets temporary amnesia about how you got their name, you just pull out the piece of paper that has permission on it. Some ISPs have become very strict, with little to zero tolerance. They can and will shut

Lastly, make sure every message you send provides instructions, or preferably an automatic means, for the recipient to opt-out of the list. If someone requests to be excluded, remove him from the list ASAP!

Quick guide to building an opt-in list:

Stage 1

In the first stage, you have identified a target audience. Let's stay with dog owners. I prefer Old English Sheepdogs myself, but let's stay with the more generic category, dog owners. I've suggested a cumulative total of 3,000 dog owners that will be targeted in three different media. Obviously, there are far more than 3,000 dog owners out there, but we'll be conservative.

Stage 2

Next, find places where these folks would normally be drawn to for information. Your own content-oriented site would be my favorite, or an e-zine that focuses on the needs of dog owners. You can also find numerous free places to advertise. Ruth, in Vestal NY, has a website www.lifestylespub.com where she categorizes and catalogs all the e-zines that are available. She tells you who the readers are (ie, dog lovers, teachers, etc) and the average number of readers. For $100, you can get a year's subscription to this site.

As well, you want to optimize your own destination or home page so that people can find you on the search engines. A great place to learn more about search engine placement is Robin Nobles' and Susan O'neil's, Maximize Web Site Traffic: Build Web site Traffic Fast and Free by Optimizing Search Engine Placement, or Fredridk Marckini's book, Search Engine Positioning: Grow Your Web Site Traffic by Achieving Top 10 Search Engine Rankings.

Again, we'll assume that the average monthly readership or visitors to each place is 1,000. Let's assume a click-through response rate of 1%, so that each location yields 10 prospects, for a total of 30.

Stage 3

Here's where you really start leveraging your time. An autoresponder is nothing more than a sophisticated email address. Think of it as your automated electronic employee, working for you 24/7/365. At predetermined times, the autoresponder automatically sends out your pre-formatted messages to people that have responded to ads, search engine inquiries, e-zine placements, web site articles, referrals, etc.

Let's say your advertisement was for a free canine-related newsletter you publish. If the respondent replies, they'll also receive a free report on the care and feeding of miniature, small, medium and large breed dogs. When they click, the autoresponder automatically sends the report as an email.

Stage 4

One of two things also happens. The first might be that a web form pops up immediately to collect their name address, telephone, email address and other qualifying information. A form is nothing more than an electronic version of a piece of paper where you gather information. For example, see the form I use to collect information on business opportunity seekers at www.Iqreply.com/aboutyou.

The second possibility is that the respondent is redirected to your own content rich web site, or even someone else's. This is a "softer" direct approach because not only are they getting a free report, they also just discovered a great information packed site to come back to. They get more bang for their click. At your web site, they can browse around and read to their heart's delight on every conceivable topic related to dog owners. Here is also where they would fill out the same type of form mentioned above.

Stage 5

The autoresponder collects, stores and puts into database fashion format every name that is submitted. That database then contains your opt-in list of names of like-minded people, in this case dog owners.

The autoresponder also keeps track of when messages have been sent out and when to send any follow up messages. Marketers know it takes somewhere between 7 to 10 communications with a prospective client before the prospect will buy. That's what the autoresponder does with those preformatted messages. The first message was the free report. You preprogram the autoresponder to send out another message in, say 3 days, then 5 days, then 2 days, then 7 days. This is what I call following up on a "regular irregular" basis. In other words, don't make the delivery of the message an expected event. It's that

On a ratio of three to one, send out three informational messages to one "soft-sell" message. The "soft-sell" message is primarily informational, but couched inside the message is some promotional content. For example, you might have sent out three messages about the grooming habits of various breeds. The fourth message might also be about grooming, but it suggests a site where they can go to get grooming tools. Maybe that's your site or an affiliate's (see number 4 below). It's a soft sell, but one that educates as well. Be sure to include you name and email on each letter that is sent. In this way, you make yourself more accountable and earn the trust of those that

Permission-Based Email Marketing

You now have a database of names of "like-minded" individuals. They've given you permission to stay in touch with them, so do that via email. This would be like the program above where you send out emails at a ratio of three informational messages to one info-mational message. And you would regularly irregularly feed them into the funnel of your web site. See the last section in this chapter.

Let's briefly review the three types of email marketing:

1. Direct email: Direct email involves sending a promotional message in the form of an email. It might be an announcement of a special offer, for example.

2. Retention email: Instead of promotional email designed only to encourage the recipient to take action (buy something, sign-up for something, etc.), you might send out retention emails. These usually take the form of regular emails known as newsletters. A newsletter may carry promotional messages or advertisements, but will aim at developing a long-term impact on the readers. It should provide the readers with value, which means more than just sales messages. It should contain information that informs, entertains or otherwise

3. Advertising in other people's emails: Instead of producing your own newsletter, you can find newsletters published by others and pay them to put your advertisement in the emails they send their subscribers. Indeed, there are many email newsletters that are created for just this purpose - to sell advertising space to others. As people tire of getting sales messages via email, it's these quality communications that perhaps hold the most potential for the future.

According to a 2001 study by New Century Communications and AdRelevance, the average costs per message were as follows:

- Permission-based direct email: $0.20
- Telemarketing: $1.00 to $3.00
- Direct mail: $0.75 to $2.00

As you can see, permission-based direct email beats all other direct-marketing vehicles hands down because there are no production, paper, or postage costs.

InternetVIZ reported in 2002 that email marketing response rates outpace direct mail ten to one. DoubleClick found in its 2002 survey that more than 88% of online consumers have made a purchase as a result of receiving email that they have requested. And, according to the Association for Interactive Marketing, 64% of surveyed marketers say that revenue has increased directly from transactions resulting from email usage.

Scandinavian Airlines (SAS) wanted to fill up some available seats during off-peak days during the holidays and had a great idea. For a special low fare of $149, SAS was offering a deal: fly out of the United States on a red eye, land in Copenhagen the next morning. Shop all day and board the plan that night. You snooze on the plane and wake up refreshed. They even gave a free shower voucher to use in the airport.

So, how did they get the word out without spending a fortune, which would in essence nullify the inexpensive package? Simply put: email based marketing. Or, better yet, viral marketing. Which is exactly what happened. For instance, after a friend received the offer in the email, she ran around telling all her friends about it and forwarded that email to about sixty people! When the email based marketing piece launched to SAS's registered user database, along with a link to the online offer and ticket purchase available online, reservations started coming in 9 minutes later and the flight packages sold out less

Affiliate Programs

OK, let's stay with our target audience of dog owners. So you log onto one of the search engines and enter the keywords, "dog owner" and "affiliate program". Make sure you include the quotes. Up will pop numerous sites that

        a. cater to the interests of dog owners and
        b. have affiliate programs you can become a member of.

I came up with 89 "hits" when I entered those words into the Google search engine.

Affiliate programs are nothing more than referral-based marketing arrangements where you get paid to refer people to other sites. For example, if you referred your database of dog owners to a web site that specialized in dog supplies, you would share in the proceeds of any resulting sales.

Another affiliate example is provided by Amazon.com. If you see a button for them at a site that is not Amazon.com itself, chances are that that other web site owner participates in Amazon.com's affiliate program. So if you were to click on that merchants Amazon.com button and bought a book or other merchandise, that referring merchant would share in the proceeds of the sale.

You can also search for affiliate programs at sites that specialize in rating affiliate programs for profitability, as well as standings against other like web sites and affiliate program directories. Here are some sites you may want to check out:

        www.associateprogram.com
        www.affiliatematch.com
        www.marketingtips.com
        www.sitesell.com
        www.cj.com (Commission Junction)

If there's one common thread that runs through most successful affiliate web sites, it's that each Webmaster has a passion for their subject matter. The right affiliate program can turn a hobby web site into something with a life (and a revenue stream) all on its own. What could be better than being paid to do something you love to do?

A prime example of this is the owner of The Flick Filosopher, which was launched in September 1997. The Flick Filosopher has original movie reviews and affiliate links. In order to derive income, each review contains direct links to the specific movie at Reel.com, so that readers can immediately purchase the film in DVD or video tape format (new or used), as well as movie soundtracks in CD format. Most reviews feature a host of relevant text links to other related movie reviews on the site, as well as to actor-specific links. The Flick Filosopher's biggest successes stem from special review themes. Reviews of television movies from the A&E, HBO, Showtime, and TNT networks provide content that's hard to find elsewhere. Mining the niches pays off. Affiliate links to Reel.com's massive inventory allow readers to easily purchase made-for-TV movies, which might otherwise

Niche Marketing

Just as it's absolutely vital to have a puzzle picture in place while solving a puzzle, carving a niche for your business is an absolute MUST for today's successful Internet business. A niche can be defined as a small targeted and focused area of any business entity that offers a unique program, or benefit, satisfying a common NEED of like-minded people.

Identifying a niche requires a particular mindset. You can't come up with a niche in a flash until you really understand how to go about it. You can only come up with a well-defined niche by having the right attitude towards a concrete, and clear objective.

You need to go through a certain hierarchy in order to find your niche. For example, if you're targeting women in business, your hierarchy may well be drawn something like this... women -> women's health -> pregnancy -> nutritional requirement in pregnancy -> semi liquid food supplement -> finally your product, with a clear and distinct benefit.

Be as specific as possible. Put your entire force towards a single specific value driven business model, rather than getting generalized and trying to sell everything under one roof. In simple terms, by narrowing your business focus you'll effectively broaden sales. You'll end up making more money this way.

And in this way, you will establish yourself as an expert in your field. To be an expert you don't necessarily need to have lot of knowledge or expertise. Needless to say you can get started right away with what you already know or enjoy doing in your spare time, and preferably have a passion for it too. Just try to be a little bit "different" than the rest.

Once you have positioned yourself online as an expert in a specific niche, you will outgrow automatically into more related profitable areas. Your credibility in such areas will carry more weight than if you would attempt to offer "everything under one roof" approach.

Another great benefit of having a narrow niche is the fact that visitors to your site will have a greater interest in what you offer. Why? Because your product or service is highly targeted to them, and you aim to solve their specific problem. What this means is your visitors are pre-qualified with a ready to buy attitude, i.e., they are almost already 50-60% convinced. The rest is your job. Make your Web site simple and attractive with a killer copy, and with useful content that further persuades them to make a purchase.

It really makes no sense starting or running an Internet business without identifying a niche. If you're really determined to get success on the Net, this is the way to go. Do some positive brainstorming, relate different things around you trying to get into a specific niche, and add value. You will eventually come up with a great idea. And a great idea is the spark for a big explosion.

One Internet marketer started out online with a generalized marketing site that was lucky to get 500 visitors a month regardless of the amount of promotion. Then, he did an in-depth review of HTML compilers for potential ebook self-publishers and the traffic increased substantially! So substantially, in fact, that he began working exclusively with ebook marketing and created www.ebooksnbytes.com. He then chose complimentary affiliate programs for marketing ebooks, HTML compilers, pricing surveys like the new "Make Your Price Sell," and other ebook-related programs, and all were much more successful at generating sales than from his previous site. Visitors increased from several hundred to almost 10,000 per month in the space of only a few

The point I am trying to get across is that by analyzing your own site's statistics, you may notice that you are sitting on a potential gold mine without even realizing it. Which page on your site is getting the most visits? Does it happen to be a page giving away free ebooks or software?

Take an honest look at your own site. Is it unique compared to many other sites out there? Do you have any original and helpful free content to attract visitors? What areas of your site are the most popular? Capitalize on those pages by featuring them or even creating separate domains with those target markets. Whether you will be catering to ezine publishers, web designers, people wanting to lose weight, or even dog breeders, all can be excellent target markets to cater to. Another benefit to niche marketing is that you may end up being ranked high on search engines without much effort since your pages will be specific as well as content-rich.

To summarize: Analyze site traffic… pick your most popular topics and specialize in those areas by building a highly informative site around that specialty. Whether it is golfing, nutritional supplements, ebooks, babies, or even snorkeling… there are affiliate programs and books that you could sell on the side for extra income. Be an expert in a topic you love and know well (or learn as much as you can about it) and then go for it!

Your Own Web Site Must Act Like a Funnel

A funnel? Why are we talking about funnels? Let me explain by first looking at the definition of a funnel: "A conical utensil having a small hole or narrow tube at the apex and used to channel the flow of a substance." Now, let's imagine that you have a funnel that is floating out there in Internet space. With any of your Internet marketing, you are trying to capture consumers and put them into your funnel.

Of course, there is no real funnel, nor are you really "capturing" anyone. You are, however, doing all that you can do to capture email addresses and add them to your database. Once that database has been established (and continues to grow, of course), what are you going to do with the names? Send information and sell products!!

With the funnel concept, you start out small and move them down the funnel to larger and more profitable products. Do these products have to be your own? No! Consider affiliate products or products you have licensed from someone else. Once you get a consumer's email and get them to buy the first product, you use your autoresponder to send them 2 more informational pieces and then another product message. If the first item they purchased exceeded their expectations, then they are more likely to purchase another item from you.

And so it goes, one item after another, until you have "groupies" that purchase just about anything you send their way. In fact, they may want to talk with you individually and see you as a guru. Consider Tony Robbins. He gets $1 million to be a personal coach! Now, I am not saying that you necessarily want to get as big as all that, but you can turn the marketing around so that you become the hunted rather than the hunter. The funnel will get people seeking you out for your skills and expertise.

Another way to gain their trust, beyond providing exceptional information is by giving a clear, no questions asked guarantee. Here's mine:

You have an unconditional, lifetime, no questions asked, 100% money back guarantee! YOU ARE NEVER AT RISK! **(By the way, not one person has yet to call!)**

Beyond all of the Internet techniques suggested in this chapter, there is simply your own website. And your website can be another avenue to gain emails to put into your funnel. Your site needs to be informative and be "them-focused." Your site can offer free stuff, which is an easy way to collect an email address and also provides an easy way for someone else to recommend your site to their friends: "Hey, Joe, I got this free report about Internet Marketing Techniques that is really great. Just go to www.reallygreatwebsite.com and get a

By the way, referred customers are more likely to buy. Why? They aren't taking your word for it, but the word of someone they know and trust that has used your product!!

For help with website promotion, go to
www.searchenginecommando.com

For help producing your own seminars, go to
http://www.webmarketingmagic.com

Bibliography:

Ackerman, Ernest C. and Karen Hartman. The Information Specialist's Guide to Searching and Researching on the Internet and the World Wide Web. (Franklin, Beedle & Assoociates, 2000)

Ackermann, Ernest C. and Karen Hartman. Searching and Researching on the Internet and the World Wide Web. (Franklin, Beedle & Assoociates, 2000)

Algie, Bob. How to Activate Your Web Site. (Que, 1999)

Allen, Robert G. Multiple Streams of Internet Income: How Ordinary People Make Extraordinary Money Online. (New York: John Wiley & Sons, 2001)

Ause, Wayne. Instant HTML Web Pages. (Ziff Davis Press, 1995)

Barksdale, Karl. HTML Activities: Webtop Publishing on the Superhighway. (Soutwestren Publishing, 1997)

Basch, Reva and Mary Ellen Bates. Researching Online for Dummies. (Hungry Minds, 2000)

Bride, Mac. HTML: Publishing on the World Wide Web (Teach Yourself) (Teach Yourslef, 1998)

Bond, Robert E. Hits! Maximizing Search Engine Hits. (Source Book Publications, 2001)

Bruemmer, Paul Joseph. #1 Search Engine Primer. (Web Ignite Corporation, 1999)

Bryant, Staphanie Cottrell. Teach Yourself HTML 4. (IDG Books Worldwide, 1999)

Burgett, Gordon. Niche Marketing for Writers, Speakers, and Entrepreneurs: How to Make Yourself Indispensable, Slightly Immortal, and Lifelong Rich in 18 Months! (Communication Unlimited, 1993)

Burns, Joe. HTML Goodies. (MacMillan Publishing Co., 1998)

Callihan, Steve. Create Your First Web Page In a Weekend. (Prima Publishing, 1999)

Carey, Patrick. New Perspectives on Creating Web Pages with HTML - Updated. (Course Technology, 1999)

Castro, Elizabeth. HTML 4 for the World Wide Web: Visual QuickStart Guide. (Peachpit Press, 1999)

Chase, Larry and Eileen Shulock. Essential Business Tactics for the Net. (New York: John Wiley & Sons, 2001)

Coleman, Pat and Anamary Ehlen (Editors) HTML Complete. (Sybex, 2000)

Cook, Rod. Rod Cook's How To Start Your Network Marketing Or Internet Multi-Affiliate Company. (America's MLM Consultants, 1999)

Curphey, Marianne. E-cash: Put Your Money Where Your Mouse Is. (Pearson Professional Education, 2000)

DeUlloa, John R. Search Engines: The Step By Step to Successfully Promoting a Web Site. (Wire Bound Photocopies, 1999)

Dunn, Declan. Complete Insiders Guide to Associate and Affiliate Programs: Discover How to Dramatically Increase Your Revenues Through Quick, Strategic Positioning on the Internet. (Adnet International, 1998)

Dunn, Delcan. Net Profits: How to Win the Internet Game: Proven Success of the $65,000 Affiliate, the $750,000 Super Affiliate, and the $600,000/6-Week Performance Network. (Adnet International, 2000)

Dunn, Delcan. Winning the Affiliate Game: The Ten-Step Master Plan for Maximizing Your Profits. (Adnet International, 1999)

Eddy, Sandra E. HTML in Plain English. (Hungry Minds, due June 2001)

Eddy, Sandra E. XHTML in Plain English. (Hungry Minds, 2000)

Evans, Tim. SAMS Teach Yourself HTML 4 in 10 Minutes. (SAMS, 1999)

Evoy, Ken. Go to www.sitesell.com

Galon, Derek. The Savvy Way to Successful Website Promotion: Secrets of Successful Websites: Attracting On-Line Traffic: The Most Up to Date Guide to Top Positioning on Search Engines. (Trafford Publishing, 1999)

Gertler, Nat and Rod Underhill. The Complete Idiot's Guide to Making Millions on the Internet. (Indianapolis, IN: Que, 2000)

Godin, Seth. Permission Marketing: Turning Strangers Into Friends And Friends Into Customers. (Simon & Schuster; 1999)

Gould, Cheryl. Searching Smart on the World Wide Web: Tools and Techniques for Getting Quality Results. (Library Solutions Press, 1998)

Gray, Daniel. The Complete Guide to Associate & Affiliate Programs on the Net: Turning Clicks Into Cash. (New York: McGraw-Hill Professional Publishing, 1999)

Gurian, Phil. E-mail Business Strategies & Dozens of Other Great Ways to Take Advantage of the Internet. (Grand National Press, 2001)

Hardaway, Glenn. Internet Income in Plain English. (Glenn Hardaway, 1996)

Helmstetter, Greg and Pamela Metivier. Affiliate Selling: Building Revenue on the Web. (New York: John Wiley & Sons, 2000)

Hinshaw, Donna and Donna M. Hinshaw. E-Commerce: Internet-Enable Your Cash Flow. (Pelican Associates, 1999)

Hock, Randolph. The Extreme Searcher's Guide to Web Search Engines: A Handbook for the Serious Searches. (Information Today, 1999)

Horton, William K., Lee Taylor, Arthur Ignacio, Nancy L. Hoft. The Web Page Design Cookbook: All the Ingredients You Need to Create 5-Star Web Pages. (New York: John Wiley & Sons, 1995)

Kelly, Jason. The Neatest Little Guide to Making Money Online. (New York: Penguin Group, 2000)

Kennedy, Renee and Terry Kent. Search Engine Optimization and Placement: An Internet Marketing Course for Webmasters. (Universal Publishers, 2001)

Kent, Gordon. Internet Publishing with Acrobat: A Comprehensive Reference for Creating and Integrating PDF Files with HTML on the Internet or Intranets. (Adobe Press Systems, 1996)

Kinnard, Shannon. Marketing With Email: A Spam-Free Guide to Increasing Awareness, Building Loyalty, and Increasing Sales By Using the Internet's Most Powerful Tool. (Maximum Pr, 1999)

Larry, Bannin K. and Bannin K. Larry, Jr. and Harold Gregg. Webmasters' Secret Internet Marketing & Search Engine Positioning Strategies. (American Media Publishers, 1999)

Laudon, Kenneth. How to Create Web Pages Using HTML. (McGraw-Hill, 1999)

Lemay, Laura and Denise Taylor. SAMS Teach Yourself Web Publishing with HTML 4 in 21 Days with CD-ROM, Professional Reference Edition. (SAMS, 2000)

Liautaud, Bernard. E-Business Intelligence: Turning Information into Knowledge into Profit. (New York: McGraw-Hill, 2000)

Lowe, Doug. Creating Web Pages For Dummies: Quick Reference Guide. (Hungry Minds, 1999)

Mack, E. Stephen and Janan Platt. HTML 4.0: No Experience Required. (Sybex, 1997)

MacPherson, Kim. Permission-Based E-Mail Marketing That Works! (Dearborn Trade Publishing, 2001)

Marckini, Fredrick. Search Engine Positioning: Grow Your Web Site Traffic by Achieving Top 10 Search Engine Rankings. (Republic of Texas Press, 2001)

Maze, Susan and Donna J. Smith. Authoritative Guide to Web Search Engines. (Neal-Schuman Publishers, 1997)

McFedries, Paul. The Complete Idiot's Guide To Creating A Web Page. (Indianapolis, IN: Que, 2000)

Millennium, Platinum. Million Dollar E-Mails: The guide to creating effective, persuasive Internet e-mail marketing campaigns that actually increase sales and work! (Platinum Millennium, 2002)

Miller, Michael. The Complete Idiot's Guide to Online Search Secrets. (Indianapolis, IN: Que, 1999)

Miller, Sam. Searching the World Wide Web: An Introductory Curriculum for Using Search Engines. (International Society for Technology in Education, 1998)

Niederst, Jennifer and Richard Koman. Learning Web Design: A beginner's Guide to HTML, Graphics and Beyond. (O'Reilly & Associates, 2001)

Nobles, Robin and Susan O'Neil. Streetwise: Maximize Web Site Traffic: Build Web Site Traffic Fast and Free by Optimizing Search Engine Placement. (Holbrook, MA: Adams Media Corporation, 2000)

Oliver, Dick and Charles Ashbacher. SAMS Teach Yourself HTML and XHTML in 24 Hours. SAMS, 2001)

Perry, Greg. HTML 4.01 Weekend Crash Course. (IDG Books Worldwide, 2000)

Pfaffenberger, Bryan. Discovering HTML 4. (Harcourt Brace & Co., 1998)

Price, Gary. The Invisible Web: Uncovering Information Sources Search Engines Can't See. (Information Today, due out July 2001)

Ray, Deborah S. and Eric J. Ray. HTML 4 for Dummies: Quick Reference. (Hungry Minds, 2000)

Rebholz, Gary. How to Use HTML and XHTML. (SAMS, 2001)

Roberts, Stevan, et. al. Internet Direct Mail: The Complete Guide to Successful E-Mail Marketing Campaigns. (McGraw-Hill Trade, 2000)

Roebuck, Michael S. A Beginner's Guide to Search Engine Placement and Ranking. (Buy Books on the Web.com, 2000)

Rosenoer, Jonathan, Douglas Armstrong and J. Russell Gates. The Clickable Corporation: Successful Strategies for Capturing the Internet Advantage. (Free Press 1999)

Samuels, H. Raymond II. Money Making E-Commerce Strategies: Revenue Sharing Affiliate Programs. (The Agora Cosmopolitan, 2001)

Sekhar, Chandra. Internet Marketing And Search Engine Positioning - A "Do It Yourself" Guide. (Southern Publishing Group, 2001)

Smith, Bud E. and Arthur Bebak. Creating Web Pages for Dummies. (Foster City, CA: IDG Books Worldwide, 2000)

Sonnenreich, Wes and Tim MacInta. Web Developer.COM Guide to Search Engines. (New York: John Wiley & Sons, 1998)

Sosinsky, Barrie and Elisabeth Parker. The Web Page Recipe Book. (ISBN: 013460296X)

Spott, Roger. Unlocking the Secrets of Internet Search Engine Ranking. (Biomed General, 2000)

Stanek, William Robert. Increase Your Web Traffic in a Weekend. (Prima Communications, 2000)

Sterne, Jim and Anthony Priore. Email Marketing: Using Email to Reach Your Target Audience and Build Customer Relationships. (John Wiley and Sons, 2000)

Tittel, Ed, Natanya Pitts, Natanya Pitts-Moultis, Chelsea Valentine and Mike Wooldridge. HTML For Dummies. (Hungry Minds, 2000)

Wayner, Peter. Digital Cash: Commerce on the Net. (Morgan Kaufmann, 1997)

Weinman, Lynda and William Weinman. Creative HTML Design.2. (Indianapolis, IN: New Riders Publishing, 2000)

Willard, Wendy. HTML: A Beginner's Guide. (New York: McGraw-Hill, 2000)

www.amazingformula.com

www.cyberwave.com

www.marketingtips.com

Self-Publishing

Forget four-color glossy brochures. Instead, spend time writing, producing, and printing your own book. Picture this. You have a book completed and printed on your topic of expertise. No matter who else is in the market, I'm 99.9% certain you will be the only one in the market who has written a book specifically on your topic. Since you have written the book, you are now the expert.

Who is going to publish your book? You are. You will self publish your book. How much will it cost? It depends on how many copies you print, how many pages you write and how fancy you make the cover and binding. Keep in mind that your book becomes one of your most effective pieces of promotional material. You may also use the book as your least expensive front end product for your funnel (See Chapter 15).

Three Ways to Write a Book

If you don't have the luxury of taking an extended working vacation, you may want to consider the next few options.

25X4X2 System

Take your topic of expertise. Ask yourself what are the 25 most important main topics regarding this subject matter. Then ask yourself to come up with approximately four subtopics for each of these main 25 topics. Write two pages per night on each of these subtopics. You will end up with a 200-page book in just over three months.

The One Page per Topic System

I know someone that used this system to put together a book on marketing. He had many ideas that he wanted to share with people so he brainstormed ideas and wrote down every single marketing idea that came to mind. He then wrote something on each topic. Some topics had short "blurbs" and others had five or six pages. After writing, he put the topics into categories that made sense. At the end of this exercise, he had a 265-page book filled with great marketing

Transcribe the Seminar System

This method is particularly effective for those of you who have difficulty writing. I assume that if you don't particularly like writing, you prefer speaking. That being the case, get six or eight of your favorite friends together, sit them down in a nice room, serve cocktails and deliver a seminar. Make sure you have thoroughly outlined your topic and have divided your presentation into bite size "modules." These will end up being your chapters when all is said and done.

The next big trick is finding someone who will transcribe the tapes for you at a reasonable price. Where can you find someone like this? Start at the local college or university. Next try the senior citizen centers. You would be amazed at the kinds of resources out there if you just start to look. Another resource you may want to check on the web is Hiredhand.com. These folks charge a certain amount of money per page.

Getting Your Book Edited

The biggest problem most people have is editing. This is simply a psychological block, especially if you feel you have to make everything perfect. This is an impossible task. Just get your thoughts down on paper and hire an editor to clean up your mess.

The best place to find inexpensive editors is, as I mentioned above for transcribers, your local college or university. Ask to speak to the English or Journalism departments. Then let the various secretaries of these departments know that you are looking for student editors. Unless things are different in your part of the country, student editors are inexpensive.

The Next Step

The most cost-effective way to get the book printed is to provide the printer with a CAMERA READY copy of your manuscript. (Talk to your printer to find out what they need). Or you can provide your manuscript to the printer on a disk, typed in a common word processing program like Microsoft Word or Corel WordPerfect. Or, if you don't have access to a computer you can have typewritten pages digitized (a process that scans typewritten documents into a computer). There is a fee for taking your manuscript off a disk and preparing it for production. This is referred to as typesetting or layout.

Shop around. Get quotes from at least three different printers. Check out their previous work. Just because they're cheaper doesn't always mean you're going to get a quality product. Once you find a printer, be sure to get a contract. This will help to ensure that your expectations are met, i.e. price, delivery, specifications.

Find a book you like the looks of. Publishing starts with the appearance of the cover. Model your publication after it. Check with the printer you decide to use. They can help you in this area.

So, how many copies should you print? You have 3 main options:

- Print 2,000 - 5,000 books at a reasonable unit price.
- Print 500 - 1,000 books at a higher unit price.
- Print covers ahead of time and copy your text on demand. This will provide you a competitive unit price with low, up-front costs.

What factors will affect the cost?

- Book dimensions (6"x 9", 81/2 x 11", etc.)
- Type of binding (perfect binding, hard bound, comb-bound, saddle stitched, velo-bound, wire-o-bound)
- Kind of paper used for the cover
- Number of ink colors on cover, and in text.
- Number of pages in text (count title page, table of contents, index, each and every page)
- Quantity of books desired.

Copyrights and ISBN

Once you write and register the manuscript, you will own the copyright to the material. It's a matter of filling out a form and sending the required fee to the U.S. Copyright Office at http://lcweb.loc.gov/copyright/

ISBN numbers are a unique number assigned to books and publishers, which are assigned and maintained by the ISBN Agency. This number is useful for consumers when trying to locate books. It is also necessary if you want to sell your books in bookstores. For more information about ISBN numbers contact the U.S. ISBN Agency at http://www.isbn.org/standards/home/isbn/us/index.asp

Self Published Bestsellers

Here are some bestsellers you may have heard of that were self published:

What Color is Your Parachute by Richard Nelson Bolles has sold over 8 million copies.

ZAPP! The Lightning of Empowerment, created by Bill Byham, is written for managers about empowering employees. It was so successful, that employees wanted their own copies! 275,000 copies sold *before* commercial publication, with more than 1.5 million sold to date.

The Lazy Man's Way to Riches was written by Joe Karbo. Using full-page ads in newspapers, he attracted sales from all over the world. Joe's investment was less than $3,000 and he sold nine million dollars worth -- and it was *never* in a bookstore!

The One-Minute Manager by Ken Blanchard and Spencer Johnson was self-published this book for their seminars, perfecting it based on feedback from seminar participants. After sales of 20,000 copies, they allowed a trade publishing company to turn the book into a bestseller.

"Feed Me, I'm Yours" is a collection of kid-tested recipes. It was rejected by 49 publishers before author Vicky Lansky decided to self-publish. It sold 300,000 copies in the self-published version. Bantam took it over and merchandized a whopping 8 million more!

Butter Busters, a health reference/cookbook title by Pam Mycoskie, has sold over 400,000 copies from her one-woman company located in Dallas.

Consider what Fred Cockfield did. After 15 years as a teacher and music store owner, he conveyed his methods in a self published book titled: Power Tools For String Bass. He sold copies of his 70-page book to customers and students. The book took off creating a buzz in the music industry.

Attorney John Graham, decided writing a book would help promote his personal injury practice. Packaged with a beautiful cover design, he printed 10,000 copies to give away to chiropractors who in turn gave the complimentary copy to their customers. This became so popular in the chiropractic community that requests were rolling in for his book, eventually drawing the media's attention. John admits that the benefits of publishing a book far exceeded his expectations and was an extremely profitable way to promote his business. No amount of investment in space advertising could have yielded him the results his book created.

Other Publications Besides a Book:

Create Your Own Newsletter

You need to have a regular outlet for all of your great ideas. As you go through the month, have one document on the computer with the name of that month's newsletter. As you get great ideas, keep dumping them into that file. By the time it comes to doing your newsletter, you will have most of your ideas stuffed into this computer document and virtually ready to go. All you'll have to do is flesh out the material and put it into some logical order.

I suggest you make the newsletter eight pages long. Anything less than this amount looks too flimsy. Anything greater than this amount is too difficult to do on a monthly basis. Remember, if you commit to doing a monthly newsletter and people pay for it, you have to deliver.

In order to make your newsletter easier to do, you can include a fair amount of samples of various things and then give your critique on each piece. Not only is it easier and quicker to do, it is more valuable for your readers. They would rather see examples and your critique than just read your brilliant information and advice. Take a look at Elaine Floyd's book called **Marketing with Newsletters** for more ideas on this important topic.

Your ezine, in whichever format you choose to use, should have information that's both well researched and documented. It should be of value to your customers and subscribers... The more information you can supply the better. The last thing you ever want to do is pass on misinformation, or outdated information. It can be in any of the following forms:

Articles- You can feature articles written either by yourself or other on-line marketers or specialists in a specific field. Keeping in mind this should be timely and of interest to the majority of your readers. Try to feature at least one of your own articles occasionally. This will help give you creditability as well as recognition in your field of expertise. If your not up to writing your own articles try to add an editorial comment outlining the content of each issue.

Special Features- This can come from a number of different resources and changes in each issue. An example of this type of content would be "THOUGHT FOR THE DAY" or "TIP OF THE DAY"

Information via Auto responder- This method allows you to reach into your readers mailbox yet again. The more times your message is put in front of your subscriber/customer the better. This also gives you a list of interested prospects for future contact.

Links- All of your content should contain links to more in depth information as well as corroboration of the information you have just presented. Also links to other web sites that offer help, software, news etc.

Advertising- If you plan to use advertising you will have several options to consider:

* Paid ads- If your subscriber base is small "500" or less, you may not be able to secure advertisers. If you want to offer advertising your best guide is to check out what similar news letters are charging and then set your rates accordingly. For a small newsletter you may want to run $5.00 ads, affordable for most, and then increase the rate when your membership grows.
* Free Advertising- You may choose to offer free advertising to your new subscribers or Barter- You can put forward a barter system for example, offer free 60 word ad's. to each subscriber that brings in 5 new subscribers. These should be subscribers that you confirm as legitimate. This can be an easy way to help you build your membership.
* Another version of this is to get your subscribers to place a link to an auto responder sample of your newsletter that they give away from there web-site. Like the following: Profit On-line:You Can Do It! Get all the home business help online for free in your email in-box every 2 weeks. For your free report: "How to sell to 99% of your web-site visitors" and subscription: Click Here and hit send. You can then follow up and attempt to bring these contacts into

Distribution methods vary. When you start out with your newsletter/ezine you may want to use your email program for distribution. Most e-mail programs such as Eudora lite and Pegasus Mail are ok for a start, but you will quickly find that as your list grows (and it will) that it becomes a huge task to maintain your subscription list on your own. A good newsletter service will do this all for YOU, leaving you to spend that time promoting your businesses, programs and your publication.

As with anything on the Internet, promotion is the key. Here is a list of links to help you promote your newsletter.

http://www.surfrealestate.com/addyour.htm

http://www.copywriter.com/lists/submit.htm

http://aae.freeservers.com/

http://www.arl.org:591/DEJsubmit/submit.html

http://certificate.net/wwio/content.htm

http://home.intekom.co.za/qualitone/wwwboard/distribute.htm

http://www.asphyxia.com/asphyxia/ezm/index_main.html

http://bizx.com/newsletter.html

http://www.coalliance.org/forms/ej.suggest.shtml

http://www.meer.net/~johnl/e-zine-list/submit.html

http://www.ezinesearch.com/search-it/ezine/

http://www.cru.fr/listes/

http://www.gizmonet.com/pubform.htm

http://certificate.net/wwio/net8.htm

http://www.dominis.com

http://www.rhoram.com/newsnet2.html

http://scout.cs.wisc.edu/scout/index.html

http://catalog.com/vivian/intsubform2.html

http://liszt.com/

http://www.thenewsstand.com/promote.htm

http://listserv.nodak.edu/

http://www.neosoft.com/internet/paml/index.html

http://www.list-city.com/subform.htm

http://home.earthlink.net/~blitop3/

http://www.linkomatic.com/articles/newsletter.cgi?10406

http://www.newsletteraccess.com/

http://www.zinerack.com/enterurl.html

http://www.tipworld.com/

http://www.directezines.com/

http://thetransom.com/chip/zines/index.html

http://www.homeincome.com/search-it/ezine/ezine-add.html

http://www.cyberprosper.com

http://www.ezinefactory.co.za/ezinelist.htm

http://www.etext.org/services.shtml

http://www.disobey.com/low/addere.shtml

http://inkpot.com/submit/

http://www.catalog.com/vivian/intsubform2.html

http://www.lifestylespub.com/

http://www.oblivion.net/zineworld/

http://www.ezine-news.com/

http://www.coalliance.org/

http://gort.ucsd.edu/newjour/submit.html

http://www.edoc.com/jrl-bin/wilma

http://www.arl.org/scomm/edir/template.html

http://www.ezconnect.com/submit.htm

http://www.newsletter-library.com/ven.htm

http://promotefree.com

To find articles that have the same interest as you, you can go to http://liszt.com/ and do a subject search to find newsletters with the exact type of customers as yours!

Another good way to promote your newsletter is swapping ads in other newsletters or buying ads in newsletters to increase your coverage.

If you put an ezine page up on your web site be sure and use the search engines to make sure it is promoted properly. More visitors to your web site will mean more subscribers to your Publication.

Create Your Own Publication

At some point, you may want to consider starting your own niche market publication. Not only can you create a publication, you can advertise your own products and services in the publication.

Now the problem would be to attract other advertisers to a publication that had no track record. I would ask myself what I would want if I were purchasing advertising from a publication of this nature. What I would want is certainty. How do you do this?

One solution would be to offer the advertisers a "deal". They would get their ads free, and they would only pay for the number of leads they get. My feeling is that it is the responsibility of your publication to generate readership and leads; therefore it is the advertisers' responsibility to close the sale on the leads you would generate.

So you might set up an 800# with different extension numbers for each advertiser. This way people who were interested would call the 800 #, and dial the extension number. You would charge the advertisers based on a dollar amount per lead. They would then be responsible for closing the sales.

The nice thing about a publication like this is that it would break even without a single advertiser. You could use the publication as a delivery device to promote your seminars and other products, thus cutting your own cost of direct mail and space advertising with the trade publications.

At the low end of the scale you can produce a newsprint publication with a two-color cover. After printing and mailing, your cost will run around 65¢ an issue.

Low Priced Reports

Your low priced reports are the very least expensive way for people to enter your funnel because they are priced at less than $10. Take individual topics and write a very specific and detailed five to seven page report about it. The information in these reports can be topics taken directly from your book. Simply expand upon the information.

Do not put these reports together flippantly. For many people, this will be the first thing that they purchase from you. If it isn't good, it will be impossible for you to take them further into your funnel.

The key to making effective reports is to give the reader very specific "how to" information. Don't just give them a few ideas and then tell them they need to buy something else. This will backfire on you. However, at the end of the report, it is perfectly acceptable for you to suggest additional items to help them along their journey. This is also an appropriate place to suggest additional resources by others. This is where your own products and affiliate products come in!

For great examples of this type of report, take a look at the reports by Jeffrey Lant (www.jeffreylant.com). These will give you a good idea of how a report of this type should be compiled. I would suggest that you buy at least one report to use as a model for how to write and create your own.

Quick Self-Publishing Tips

1. Know why you're publishing and publish on an "in demand" topic.

2. Don't use your name in the publishing company name. Too self-serving.

3. Accept any and all kinds of payment.

4. Must provide timely and up-to-date information.

5. Pack it out with useable information and lots of how-to's.

6. Search Internet, local library, Amazon, B&N, and go to local bookstore to see what your competition is putting out for your topic.

7. Interview experts.

8. Be organized.

Glossary of Self Publishing Terms

Camera ready copy: A printed copy of your manuscript that is ready to go to press, in the proper format that is required for your printer.

Perfect Binding: A process of binding pages into a book cover. Used in production of paperback novels.

Comb-binding: A plastic "spiral" is inserted into holes drilled directly into edge of book pages. Book will open flat for easy reading.

Saddle Stitching: Usually used on smaller page quantities, book pages are "stitched" or stapled in two or three places on fold.

Velo-binding: A plastic strip along front cover. Book will NOT open flat.

Hard-bound: Hard cover book binding, usually vinyl covering over cardboard.

Bibliography:

Adler, Bill. Inside Publishing. (Indianapolis: Bobbs-Merrill Co., 1982)

Adler, Bill. The Literary Agent's Guide to Getting Published And Making Money from Your Writing. (Claren Books, 2000)

Alden, Chevy. How To Get Published-Guaranteed: A Self-Help Manual for Assuring The Publication of Your Books. (Tri-Pacer Press, 1995)

Alexander, E. Curtis (Editor). How to Publish and Market Your Own Book As an Independent Black Publisher. (E C A Associates, 1988)

Allison, Alida. The Grad Student's Guide to Getting Published. (Hungry Minds, 1992)

Alpern, Andrew. 101 Questions About Copyright Law. (Dover Publications, 1998)

Appelbaum, Judith. How To Get Happily Published. (New York: Harper Perennial, 1998)

Bailey, Mike. Writing Erotic Fiction: And Getting Published. (Teach Yourself, 1998)

Baker, Donna. Writing a Romantic Novel: And Getting Published. (Teach Yourself, 1998)

Balkin, Richard. A Writer's Guide to Book Publishing. (New York: Plume, 1994)

Barrett, John Paul. How to Make a Book: An Illustrated Guide to Making Books by Hand. (Gaff Press, 1993, ISBN: 0961962933)

Belkin, Gary S. Getting Published: A Guide For Businesspeople And Other Professionals. (Wiley Press, ISBN: 0471883077)

Bell, Patricia. The Prepublishing Handbook: What You Should Know Before You Publish Your First Book. (Cat's Paw Press, 1992)

Bentley, Nancy, Donna Guthrie and Katy Keck Anrstein. The Young Journalist's Book: How to Write and Produce Your Own Newspaper. (Millbrook Press Trade, 2000)

Bernstein, Leonard. Getting Published: The Writer in the Combat Zone. (William Morrow & Co., 1986)

Besenjak, Cheryl. Copyright Plain and Simple. (Career Press, 2000)

Best, Don and Peter Goodman. The Author's Guide to Marketing Your Book: From Start to Success, for Writers and Publishers. (Stone Bridge Press, 2001)

Black, Dolores, Sally Brown, Abby Day and Phil Race. 500 Tips for Getting Published: A Guide for Educators, Researchers and Professionals. (Kogan Page, 1998)

Blake, Stephen. The Portable Writers' Conference: Your Guide To Getting And Staying Published. (Fresno, CA: Quill Driver Books, 1997)

Blanco, Joddee. The Complete Guide to Book Publicity. (Allworth Press, 2000)

Bly, Robert W. How to Get Your Book Published: Inside Secrets of a Successful Author. (Robllin Press, 2000)

Boswell, John. The Insider's Guide to Getting Published: Why They Always Reject Your Manuscript and What You Can Do About It. (Main Street Books, 1997)

Bowker Staff. ILMP 2001: The Directory of the International Book Publishing Industry. (Bowker, 2000, ISBN: 0835243451)

Bowker Staff. Literary Marketplace 2001: The Directory of the American Book Publishing Industry with Industry Yellow Pages. (Bowker, 2000)

Brent, Bill. Make a Zine: A Guide to Self-Publishing Disguised As a Book on How to Produce a Zine. (Black Books, 1997)

Brown, A. S. The Publishing List: The Self-Publishers' Book of Essential Information. (New Park Press, 1999)

Brunnin, Brad and Peter Beren. The Writer's Legal Companion: The Complete Handbook for the Working Writer. (Perseus Books Group, 1998)

Burgett, Gordon. How to Publish Your Own Book and Earn $50,000 Profit. (Communication Unlimited, 1997)

Burgett, Gordon. How to Sell Your Book to General and Niche Markets. (Communicaiton Unlimited, 1996)

Bykofsky, Sheree and Jennifer Bayse Sander. The Complete Idiot's Guide to Getting Published. (Macmillan Distribution, 1998)

Caputo, Tony C. How to Self-Publish Your Own Comic Book: The Complete Resource Guide to the Business, Production, Distribution, Marketing and Promotion of Comic Book. (Watson-Guptil Publications, 1997)

Cardoza, Avery. The Complete Guide to Successful Publishing: How to Create, Print, Distribute, and Make Money Publishing Books. (Cardoza Publishing, 1998)

Carroll, William. Self Publishing Made Easy. (Coda Publications, 1999)

Carroll Publishing. Government Phone Book USA 1999: A Comprehensive Guide to Federal, State, County, and Local Government Offices in the United States. (Omnigraphics, ISBN: 0780803604)

Chapman, Gillian and Pam Robson. Making Books: A Step-by-Step Guide to Your Own Publishing. (Millbrook Press, 1994)

Chickadel, Charles. Publish It Yourself: The Complete Guide To Self-Publishing Your Own Book. (Trinity Press, ISBN: 0931314011)

Clark, Sherryl. Successful Self-Publishing: Making And Selling Your Own Book. (Hale & Iremonger, 1998)

Cole, David. Complete Guide to Book Marketing. (Allworth Press, 1999)

Corpening, Gene. What The Self-Publishing Manuals Don't Tell You: And You Didn't Know To Ask. (Granite Falls, NC: Alice Pub., 1995)

Crawford, Tad. Business And Legal Forms For Authors And Self-Publishers. (New York: Allworth Press, 1996)

Curran, Susan. How to Write a Book and Get It Published: A Complete Guide to the Publishing Maze. (HarperCollins, ISBN: 0722521464)

Curtis, Richard. How to Be Your Own Literary Agent: The Business of Getting a Book Published. (Houghton Mifflin, 1996)

De Abreau, Carlos. Opening the Doors to Hollywood: How to Sell Your Idea Story, Book, Screenplay, Manuscript. (Random House, 1997)

Despain, J. J. A Writer's Guide to Getting Published in Magazines. (Aletheia, 2000)

Dunn, Danielle and Jessica Dunn. A Teen's Guide To Getting Published: The Only Writers Guide Written By Teens For Teens. (Waco, TX: Prufrock Press, 1997)

Edelstein, Scott. 30 Steps to Becoming a Writer: And Getting Published: The Complete Starter Kit for Aspiring Writers. (Writers Digest Books, 1993)

Evanson, Jane and LuAnne Dowling. Breaking into Print: How to Write and Publish Your First Book. (Kendall/Hunt Publishing, 2000)

Faler, Richard E. The Complete, Authoritative Guide to Self-Publishing: Earn Money by Designing, Producing and Promoting Your Own Books, Newsletters and Magazines. (1998, ISBN: 1881399125)

Fife, Bruce. An Insider's Guide to Getting Published: How to Create Persuasive Query Letters, Convincing Book Proposals, and Winning Manuscripts; Avoid Mistakes. (Piccadilly Books, 1993)

Fishman, Stephen. The Copyright Handbook: How to Protect and Use Written Works. (Berkeley, CA: Nolo Press, 1999)

Fishman, Stephen. The Public Domain: How to Find Copyright-Free Writings, Music, Art & More. (Berkeley, CA: Nolo.com, 2001

Flashner, Mike. How to Write a Book on Your Computer. (Flashners Publishing, 1998)

Fondiller, Shirley H. Writer's Workbook: Health Professionals' Guide to Getting Published. (Jones & Bartlett Publishing, 1999)

Fordham University Graduate School of Business Administration. Book Industry Trends 2000. Published in editions. (Book Industry Study Group, 2000)

Forsythe, Patrick and Robin Birn. Marketing in Publishing. (Rutledge, 1997)

Gallagher, Patricia C. For All the Write Reasons: Forty Successful Authors, Publishers, Agents and Writers Tell You How to Get Your Book Published. (Young Sparrow Press, ISBN: 0943135192)

Gates, A. M. Instruction Book for Writers: A Step-By-Step Guide to Publishing, Marketing and Promoting Your Book. (Cornerstone Publishing, 1995)

Gelb, Eric. Book Promotion Made Easy: Event Planning, Presentation Skills & Product Marketing. (Career Advancement Center, 2000)

German, William and William Germano. Getting It Published: A Guide for Scholars and Anyone Else Serious About Serious Books. (University of Chicago Press, Due May 2001)

Gleeck, Fred. Self-Publishing for Maximum Profit: A Step by Step Guide to Making Big Money With Your Book and Other "How To" Material. (Fast Froward Press, 2001)

Glenn, Peggy. Publicity for Books and Authors: A Do-It-Yourself Handbook for Small Publishing Firms and Enterprising Authors. (Aames-Allen, 1984)

Grant-Adamson, Lesley. Writing Crime & Suspense Fiction: And Getting Published. (Teach Yourself, 1996)

Guide to Women Book Publishers in the United States for 1990. (Clothespin Fever Press, 1990, ISBN: 0961657294)

Henderson, Kathy. Young Writers Guide to Getting Published. (Writers Digest Books, 2001)

Herman, Jeff. Writer's Guide to Book Editors, Publishers, and Literary Agents, 2001-2002: Who They Are! What They Want! And How to Win Them Over. (Prima Publishing, 2000)

Higgins, Mike. Co-Publishing: How To Get Your Book Published Now. (Boulder Mountain Press, ISBN: 1880334003)

Hoff, Barbara and Marilyn G. McFayden. Bring Out Your Own Book: Low Cost Self-Publishing. (Godiva, 1980, ISBN: 0938018000)

Holm, Kirsten. Writer's Market 2001: 8000 Editors Who Buy What You Write. (F&W Publications, 2000)

Holm, Kirsten. 2001 Writer's Market: The Internet Edition. (Writer's Digest Books, 2000)

Holt, Robert Lawrence. How to Publish, Promote, and Sell Your Own Book. (St. Martins Press, 1986)

Hubbard, Linda S. (Editor). Book Publishers Directory: A Guide to New and Established, Private and Special Interest, Avant-Garde and Alternative. (Gale Group)

Hupalo, Peter I. How To Start And Run a Small Book Publishing Company: A Small Business Guide To Self-Publishing and Independent Publishing. (HCM Publishing, 2002)

Ide, Arthur Frederick. Publishing Your Own Book. (Ide House, 1998)

Jassin, Lloyd J. and Steven C. Schechter. The Copyright Permission and Libel Handbook: A Step-by-Step Guide for Writers, Edotors and Publishers. (New York: John Wiley & Sons, 1998)

Jiloty, Joseph A. Without a Franchise Fee...I Became a Book Publisher. (Corporate Image Publishing, 1996)

Jones, Allan Frewin and Lesley Pollinger. Writing for Children: And Getting Published. (NTC Publishing Group, 1997)

Kiefer, Marie. Book Publishing Resource Guide: Complete Listings for More Than 7500 Book Marketing Contacts and Resources. (Ad-Lib Publications, ISBN: 0912411465)

Kirsch, Jonathan. Kirsch's Guide to the Book Contract: For Authors, Publishers, Editors and Agents. (Acrobat Books, 1998)

Kirsch, Jonathan. Kirsch's Handbook of Publishing Law: For Author's, Publishers, Editors and Agents. (Acrobat Books, 1994)

Kozak, Ellen M. Every Writer's Guide to Copyright and Publishing Law. (Henry Holt & Co., 1997)

Kozak, Ellen M. From Pen to Print: The Secrets of Getting Published Successfully. (Henry Holt, 1992)

Kremer, John. 1001 Ways to Market Your Books. (Open Horizons, 2001)

Lant, Jeffrey E. E-Mail El Dorado: Everything You Need to Know to Sell More of Your Products and Services Every Day by E-Mail Without Ever Spamming Anyone. (Jeffrey Lant Associates, 1998)

Lant, Jeffrey E. How to Make a Whole Lot More Than 1,000,000 Writing, Commissioning, Publishing, and Selling How to Information. (Jeffrey Lant Associates, 1993)

Largent, R. Karl and Matthew V. Clemens. Getting Published...How the Pros Do It. (Robin Vincent Publishing, 1999)

Larsen, Michael. How to Write a Book Proposal. (Writer's Digest Books, 1997)

Lee, Robert E. A Copyright Guide for Authors. (Kent Communications, 1996)

Levin, Martin P. Be Your Own Literary Agent: The Ultimate Insider's Guide to Getting Published. (Ten Speed Press, 1999)

Levine, Mark L. Negotiating a Book Contract: A Guide for Authors, Agents and Lawyers. (Moyer Bell, 1988)

Levinson, Jay Conrad, Rick Frishman and Michael Larsen. Guerrilla Marketing for Writers : 100 Weapons for Selling Your Work. (Writers Digest Books, 2000)

Lutzer, Arnold P. Copyrights and Trademarks for Media Professionals. (Butterworth-Heinemann, 1997)

Lyon, Elizabeth. The Sell Your Novel Toolkit: Everything You Need To Know About Queries, Synopses, Marketing & Breaking In. (Hillsboro, OR: Blue Heron Publishing, 1997)

MacDonald, Janet. Writing Non-Fiction and Getting Published. (Teach Yourself, 1998)

MacKenzie, Linda. How to Self-Publish & Market Your Personal Growth Book. (Crossing Press, ISBN: 0895949814)

Marsh, Carole. Publishing on Command: How to Use Desktop Publishing to Produce a Sample of Your Book for a Publisher or a Complete Small Press Run. (Gallopade Publishing Group, 1990)

Marsh, Carole. You'd Betters!: The Rules Writers Break That Keep Them From Getting Published (& How To Stop!) (Gallopade Publishing Group, 2000)

Martin, Paul Raymond and Polly Keener. The Writer's Little Instruction Book: 385 Secrets for Writing Well and Getting Published. (Writers World Press, 1998)

Masello, Robert. Writer Tells All: Insider Secrets to Getting Your Book Published. (Wise Owl Books, 2001)

Millard, Bob. Book Production On Your Kitchen Table: A Guide For The Author/Publisher. (Brevity Press, ISBN: 0917838041)

Murphy, Donna M. The Woman's Guide To Self-Publishing: A Comprehensive Guide For Helping Women Understand And Pursue Self-Publishing. (Fort Collins, Colo.: IRIE Publications & Productions, 2000)

NPD Group. 1999 Consumer Research Study on Book PurchISBNg. (Book Industry Study Group, 2000, ISBN: 0940016761)

O'Connor, Richard F X. How to Market You & Your Book: The Ultimate Insider's Guide to Get Your Book Published With Maximum Sales. (O'Connor House Publishing, 1998)

Ortman. Mark. A Simple Guide to Marketing Your Book: What an Author and Publisher Can Do to Sell More Books. (Wise Owl Books, 1998)

Ortman, Mark. A Simple Guide to Self-Publishing: A Step-by-Step Handbook to Prepare, Print, Distribute & Promote Your Own Book. (Wise Owl Books, 2000)

Ottenstein, Claire. 7 Steps To Getting Published: An Easy Reference Book For Writers Of Poetry, Short Stories, Novels, Children's Books, Articles, Plays, Film, TV, Radio. (Counterpoint Publishing, ISBN: 1878149148)

Page, Susan. The Shortest Distance Between You and a Published Book. (Broadway Books, 1997)

Parsons, Paul. Getting Published: The Acquisition Process at University Presses. (University of Tenesee Press, 1989)

Perkins, Wayne. A Cheap and Easy Guide to Self-Publishing E-Books. (Wayne Perkins, ISBN: 1929695209)

Paul, Don. How To Write a Book in 53 Days: The Elements of Speed Writing Necessity and Benefits Too: How to Produce, Publish and Sell a Great Book. (Pathfinder Publicaitons, 1992)

Peake, Jacquelyn. Publish Your Own Book (and Pocket the Profits): A Complete Guide to Successful Self-Publishing. (2000, ISBN: 0595165400)

Pinskey, Raleigh. 101 Ways to Promote Yourself. (Avon, 1997)

Potter, Clarkson N. Who Does What And Why In Book Publishing. (Secaucus, NJ: Carol Pub. Group, 1990)

Poynter, Dan. Book Marketing; A New Approach - Photocopy Edition. (Para Publishing, 1999)

Poynter, Dan. Is There a Book Inside You?: Writing Alone or With a Collaborator. (Para Publishing, 1998)

Poynter, Dan. The Self-Publishing Manual: How to Write, Print and Sell Your Own Book. (Para Publishing, 2000)

Poynter, Dan. Successful Nonfiction: Tips and Inspiration for Getting Published. (Para Publishing, 1999)

Publishers, Distributors & Wholesalers of the United States 1999-2000. (Bowker, 1999, ISBN: 0835242617)

Raab, Susan. An Author's Guide to Children's Book Promotion. (Raab Associates, 1999)

Radke, Linda Foster. The Economical Guide to Self-Publishing: How to Produce and Market Your Book on a Budget. (Five Star Publications, 1996)

Raschack, Jason B. Comic Book Publishing. (Edutainment Media, 2000)

Reiss, Fern. The Publishing Game: Publish a Book in 30 Days. (Peanut Butter and Jelly Press, 2003)

Relova, Lisa Price. How To Self-Publish Your Own Book. (Pumpkin Publishing, 1999)

Rice, Craig S. How to Market Your Book and Get Published: Just the Nuts and Bolts. (Nova Kroshka Books, 1996, ISBN: 1560722770)

Ross, Marilyn and Tom Ross. Jump Start Your Book Sales: A Money-Making Guide for Authors, Independent Publishers and Small Presses. (Writer's Digest Books, 1999)

Ross, Marilyn Heimberg. Marketing Your Books: A Collection Of Profit-Making Ideas For Authors And Publishers. (Buena Vista, CO: Communication Creativity, 1990)

Ross, Tom and Marilyn Ross. Complete Guide to Self Publishing: Everything You Need to Know to Write, Publish, Promote, and Sell Your Own Book (Self-Publishing 4th Edition). (F&W Publications, 2002)

Rovenhauer, Madelyne Simone. The Nasty Little Writing Book: Longtime New York Publishing Insider Reveals Secrets Only Best-Selling Authors Know. (Elderberry Press, 2000) Note: Book's cover reads: "THE BOOK THAT WILL TURN *YOU* INTO A BEST-SELLING AUTHOR—*GUARANTEED*—OR FIVE TIMES YOUR MONEY BACK!"

Rubie, Peter. The Everything Get Published Book. (Adams Business Media, 2000)

Salisbury, Linda G. and Jim Salisbury. Smart Self-Publishing: An Author's Guide to Producing a Marketable Book. (Tabby House, 1997)

Seidman, Michael. Fiction: The Art and Craft of Writing and Getting Published. (Pomgranate, 1999)

Seuling, Barbara. How to Write a Children's Book and Get It Published. (Hungry Minds, 1991)

Shapiro, Ellen R. Writer's Guide to Children's Book Editors, Publishers, and Literary Agents: Who They Are! What They Want! And How to Win Them Over! (Prima Publishing, 2001)

Shelton, Connie. Publish Your Own Novel: Get Your Book into Print and into the Stores Now! (Columbine Publishing, 1997)

Shelton, Kathleen. How to Self Publish Your Book for under $500.00. (Kisco Publications, 2000)

Shinder, Jason, Amy Holman and Kathleen Adams (Editors) The First-Book Market: Where and How to Publish Your First Book and Make It a Success. (Hungry Minds, 1998)

Shinder, Jason and Jeff Herman. Get Your First Book Published: And Make It a Success. (Career Press, 2001)

Shur, Rudy. How to Publish Your Nonfiction Book: A Complete Guide to Making the Right Publisher Say Yes. (Square One Publishers, 2001)

Silverman, Robert J. Getting Published in Education Journals. (Charles C. Thomas, ISBN: 0398046220)

Smedley, Christine S. and Mitchell Alan. Getting Your Book Published. Sage Publications, 1994)

Smith, Gary Michael. Publishing for Small Press Runs: How to Print and Market from 20 to 200 Copies of Your Book. (Chatgris Press, 2001)

Smith, Sara Freeman and Mack E. Smith. How to Self-Publish & Market Your Own Book: A Simple Guide for Aspiring Writers Includes Special Section for Women & Minority Writers. (2001, ISBN: 0966232879)

Snell, Michael, Kim Baker and Sunny Baker. From Book Idea to Bestseller: What You Absolutely, Positively Must Know to Make Your Book a Success. (Prima Publishing, 1997)

Spicer, Robert. Publishing a Book : How to Publish Your Own Work and Make a Profit. (How To Books, 1998)

Stabelford, Brian. Writing Fantasy & Science Fiction: And Getting Published. (Teach Yourself, 1998)

Sterling, Cynthia and M. G. Davidson. Getting Your Manuscript Sold : Surefire Writing and Selling Strategies That Will Get Your Book Published. (Empire Publishing Service, 1995)

Stevens, Barbara. Writing and Getting Published: A Primer for Nurses. (Springer Publications, 1995)

Stim, Richard W. Getting Permission: How to License and Clear Copyrighted Materials Online and Off with Disk. (Berkeley, CA: Nolo Press, 1999)

Stoneburner, Bryan C. Self-Publishing For Fun And Profit: A Guide To Creating, Printing, And Marketing Your Own Book. (Pacific Editions, ISBN: 0963519123)

Strong, William S. The Copyright Book: A Practical Guide. (MIT Press, 1999)

Stuart, Sally E. Sally Stuart's Guide to Getting Published. (Harold Shaw, 1999)

Sweeney, Matthew, John Hartley Sweeney, John Hartley Williams and Martin Sweeney. Writing Poetry: And Getting Published. (Teach Yourself, 1998)

Talab, R. S. Commonsense Copyright: A Guide for Educators and Librarians. (McFarland & Co., 1999)

Tedder, Lorna. Book Promotion for the Shameless: 101 Marketing Tips That Really Work (3.5 Diskette) (Spilled Candy Publications, 1999)

Thomas, Suzanne P. Make Money Self-Publishing: Learn How From Fourteen Successful Small Publishers. (Boulder, CO: Gemstone House Pub., 2001)

Tucker, Bettie E and Wayne Brumagin. How to Self-Publish Your Book With Little Or No Money! A Complete Guide to Self-Publishing at a Profit! (Rainbows End Company, 2000)

Tyson, Herb. Teach Yourself Web Publishing With Microsoft Word in a Week/Book and Disk. (ISBN: 0672307642)

Underdown, Harold and Lynne Rominger. The Complete Idiot's Guide to Publishing Children's Books. (Macmillan Publishing, 2001)

Vanderbilt, Arthur T., II. The Making of a Bestseller: From Author to Reader. (McFarland & Company, 1999)

Vaughn, Patricia. Write, Publish and Market Your Book. (A Cappella Publishing, 1997)

Weimer, Joe. Writing and Selling Your Nonfiction Book (Audio). (Prairie Dog Press, 1997)

West, Michelle. The No-Bull Guide to Getting Published and Making It As a Writer: Everything You Need to Know to Break Into & Prosper in This Exciting & Lucrative Field. (Winslow Publishing, ISBN: 0921199066)

Wheeler, Helen Rippier. Getting Published in Women's Studies : An International Interdisciplinary Professional Development Guide Mainly for Women. (MacFarland & Company, ISBN: 0899504000)

Williams, Thomas A. How to Publish Local and Regional Magazines and Guidebooks. (Venture Press, 2000)

Williams, Thomas A. How to Publish Weekly Newspapers, Free Circulation Shoppers and Niche Market Tabloids. (Venture Press, 2000)

Williams. Thomas A. Poet Power! The Practical Poet's Complete Guide to Getting Published. (Venture Press, 1999)

Wimbs, Diana. Freelance Copywriting . A.C. Blac & Co., 1999)

Winget, Larry H. How To Write A Book One Page At A Time. (Win Publications, 1997)

Writer's Digest Books. Beginner's Guide to Getting Published. (Writer's Digest Books, 1994)

Yorgason, Brenton G. The Wings of Words: Writing and Publishing a Book Made Easy. (1999, ISBN: 0965955990)

Young, Jordan R. How to become a successful freelance writer : a practical guide to getting published. (Moonstone Press, ISBN: 0940410036)

Zackheim, Sarah Parsons, Adrian Zackheim and Nelson Demille. Getting Your Book Published for Dummies. (Hungry Minds, 2000)

Zoltan, Melanie Barton. A Kid's Guide to Getting Published. (Camino Books, 2001)

Network Marketing

If you don't know what Network Marketing is, it is a 50-year-old industry and has the highest residuality quotients of anything that I have shown to you or will show to you in this book. Network Marketing is just a way for businesses to distribute their products. It is:

- Person-to-person communication
- Establishing, building and nurturing relationships
- Marketing channel
- A different way of doing business
- Helping and serving other people
- A way of living: FREEDOM!
- Residual income at its best

Rather than using the customary distribution process that moves from manufacturer to warehouse to wholesaler to retailer to end customer, Network Marketing companies use a network of independent marketers to move the products directly from the manufacturer to the end customer.

Any business methodology that is not in sync with the "norm" will always be considered a scam. Network marketing, however, is not a scam but a great way to produce residual income.

The independent marketers earn a percentage of the profit on all sales they make. While it's possible and highly recommended to earn an income by selling to customers directly, the real power of Network Marketing is that you are allowed to build a downline of other independent marketers below you, and earn a percentage of their combined sales.

Success Factors

1. Company track record: How long have they been in business? Anything under 5 years, I would not touch with a ten foot pole. Chances are 95% that any network marketing company will not be around after 5 years.

2. Financially strong: You will want them to prove this.

3. Experienced management team: Do they have any prior Fortune 500 management personnel as part of their team?

4. Unique products or services.

5. Competitively priced: If they are higher priced than the typical Walmart or CVS, then the consumer had better believe that there is a higher perceived value for the product.

6. A practical, realistic personal production requirement.

7. High reorder rate from customers and builders, with an emphasis on customers.

8. Minimal start-up costs: Anything under $1000.

9. Fair compensation plan.

10. An "Anyone can do it" marketing plan.

11. Timing

12. Complete and comprehensive business training, support, and systems education—all designed, produced and distributed by the network marketing company itself.

13. No risk: A 100% money back guarantee.

14. Relationships: The person who presented to you can AND will work with you personally. Remember, this is a business of relationships!

Is There a Downside?

1. Rejection, especially from spouse, relatives and close friends.

2. Fear of prospecting, e.g., the 500 pound phone.

3. What are you doing with that? You've got a good job!

4. What will our friends say?

5. Depression.

6. Don't buy into hype. Be realistic. Tell the truth!

7. Criteria for success is different.

8. Playing "not to lose" instead of "a no matter what" attitude.

9. Changing the "system."

What Works

1. One-on-one meeting

2. Two-on-one meeting

3. "Group" meeting

4. Telephone and conference call presentations

5. Hotel meetings

6. Presentations: Your story, the company's story, describe products/services, comp plan, close.

How to Prospect and Approach Inside and Outside Your "Warm" Market and Have Fun Doing It:

1. Don't overexpose it ... keep it short and simple ... K.I.S.S.!

2. Make notes before you make a call. If it's worth doing, it's worth doing right. Always have a script in front of you!

3. Arouse curiosity. Be enthusiastic. "It's not the words you say. It's the music that you play."

4. Always carry your calendar and your contact list and cell phone. Minimum 150 current names and numbers.

5. Ask questions! The person who asks the questions controls the conversation.

6. NEVER give into someone's curiosity. If you give them a 5-minute presentation and (by mistake!) they get in, you have taught them to do the same.
7. Present to husbands and wives together, unless it is absolutely impossible.
8. Call to confirm the appointment. Call the night before AND the day of. Say, "Did we say 7:30 or 7:45?" or "Is that 1234 Main St. or 1235 Main Street?" Be on time. Be on time. Be on time. Be on time. Be on time. Be on time. Be on time! NEVER late.
9. Ask three questions as part of the follow up confirmation the night before. Were you serious about that?
10. Practice, practice, practice makes permanent, not perfect.
11. Do it now and do it often!
12. For cold calls and follow up calls, use the 4 C's"
    A. Compliment
    B. Create curiosity
    C. Control the conversation
    D. Commitment (set the appointment)
13. Have fun, but treat your business SERIOUSLY! Treat it like a business. 40 months or 40 years to financial security.
14. Always have a back-up plan in case of a cancellation. This is important so that you are always working the hours you are committed to.
15. TEAM UP! Calendaring and partnering are essential to your success. Go upline. Communication on a daily basis is crucial. Get three-way calling. Compress time.

REMEMBER!

1. The only way you will really learn how to approach is by going out and doing it.

2. In response to objections: feel, felt, found. "I understand how you feel. I felt the same way when I first heard of this. But now I found..."

3. It is said that in sales, statistically, people have to be approached 7 times before they agree to listen. Don't give up after the first time someone says "no". Remember, things change in people's lives.

4. Always give an alternate choice of "yes" or "yes."

5. Every no brings you that much closer to your next customer or builder.

6. Always ask for referrals.

Advertising

The new MLMer faces a daunting task...and competition...when it comes to "advertising". Finding that "best combination" of time, effort, and money is a growth experience. Rarely will it just appear....education (self and provided) plus mentoring (if available) are important factors and hopefully a fact of life. However, "advertising" is not impossible. How you "advertise" or "share" can take many forms. There are free and inexpensive methods that do work. It's a matter of finding those that work for you.

1. Writing and submitting ezine articles is an excellent method. It requires time & effort...but no money. The benefits include increased link popularity for the url used in your sig box (important for search engine ranking), branding, and reach (you can "reach" more with an article than an ezine ad). Plus it's viral. Often your article is archived by publishers and directories.....available well after it was originally offered. Plus publishers and web masters will often "pick up" your article...again well after you originally submitted it.

2. Business cards are always a good method...and more inexpensive than one realizes. You can even make your own. Just pass them out like candy....stores, church, ball games, local events, restaurants (leave 1 with your bill), businesses you frequent, networking meetings, local Chamber Of Commerce. The possibilities are only limited by your imagination.

3. Flyers, posters, post cards, brochures, etc. can also be done very inexpensively. You can make your own on your PC or purchase custom

or ready-made templates from numerous online providers. You could even strike up a joint venture with a local community provider. They print it for you and include their "advert" somewhere...you distribute. You both win, you pay less, and maybe influence that partner to be involved in your business.

4. Web decals on your vehicle(s) is another inexpensive method. Cost is about $40 each but the visibility is priceless.

5. Newspaper/magazine ads can be found that aren't going to cost an arm and a leg. Local publications are the best place to start. Nationwidenewspapers.com is an excellent source. For some services you may find College student newspapers and alumni magazines to be good performers.

Of course there are the traditional ezine and magazine ads, leads programs, event booths, direct mailings, card decks, Forum participation, search engines, etc. Most of these will cost you money...all will cost you time & effort.

The key I believe is in being creative and sticking to what best fits your time, effort, money combination. It is and should be a personal choice. If the dollar "cost" doesn't give you the dollar "value" you hope for, keep looking. But don't EVER give up. Plus...diversify. Use multiple methods. Why limit yourself to just "one path"?

Just remember to be honest, be helpful, be yourself....and have fun! Then pass it on!

Tips For Getting Started

1. Forget about "Getting Rich Quick!" If you're looking to "Get Rich Quick," you better take some heavy risks or be awfully lucky, because this business, like any other business, takes time and hard work. No way around it.

2. There's no secret that the network marketers making the most profits have the largest lists. The quickest way to build your list and keep in constant contact with your prospects is to publish an ezine.

3. Freebies are the best ways to generate leads and build your list. Free reports, free eBooks, free software, use any or all of these to

gather email addresses and your list will build in no time. Always make sure the prospect leaves their address in return for the freebie.

4. Build a site geared around your network marketing program in specific or MLM in general

5. Patience is the key. It takes about 1 year before true "Geometric Progression" begins to take place. It's no coincidence that:

- Most network marketers quit within the first year.
- Most network marketers fail.
- Network marketers that stick it out for a year or more usually end up becoming the new "Heavy Hitters."

6. Make a commitment to recruit a new member into your first level on a daily basis. There are two major reasons for doing this.

- Momentum is a key factor in keeping you dedicated to your efforts.
- Only about 5% of your frontline members will contribute to building your downline.

7. The majority of your time should be spent recruiting. You'll waste a lot of time trying to work with the 95% that aren't going to do anything. Offer your help and those that are serious will contact you.

8. Once you've developed your downline and your contact list, you can maximize your profits by diversifying. Multiple streams of income will take you to the next level and your monthly income will continue to grow. You can diversify by:

- Adding more programs.
- Adding webmaster tools such as autoresponders and hosting.
- Adding informational products and programs.
- Adding time saving software.

When you diversify, think in terms of related goods and services that will benefit your downline.

Bibliography:

Adams, Garrett. MLM (Multi-Level Marketing) Made Easy. (Deerfield Beach, FL: Made E-Z Products, 2000)

Amick, Charles F. Network Marketing: How To Play By Your Own Rules and Win. (Upublish Communications, 1998)

Anderton. Mary. A Great Way to Get Wealth : How to Start and Build a Network Marketing Business from Your Home. (Colonial Press, 1993)

Andrecht, Venus Catherine. MLM Magic: How I Made $100,000 In Just 10 Months!: You Can, Too! (Ramona, CA: Ransom Hill Press, 1993)

Andrecht, Venus. MLM Magic: How an Ordinary Person Can Build an Extraordinary Networking Business from Scratch. (Ramona, CA: Ransom Hill Press, 1992)

Averill, Mary. Network Marketing: The Business of the '90s. (Menlo Park, CA: Crisp Publications, 1995)

Babener, Jeffrey A. and David Stewart. The Network Marketer's Guide to Success. (Portland, OR: Legaline Press, 1990) Available at www.mlmlegal.com/books.html

Babener, Jeffrey. TAX GUIDE for MLM/Direct Selling Distributors. Available at www.mlmlegal.com/books.html

Ballard, Debbi A. How to Succeed in Your Own Network Marketing Business. (Mesa, AZ: IMLC, Inc., 1991)

Barrett, Thomas. Dare to Dream and Work to Win. (Blue Ribbon Video, 1998)

Baytes, Allen. How Secure is Your Financial Future?

Berry, Richard. Direct Selling: From Door to Door to Network Marketing. (Butterworth-Heinemann, 1997)

The Big Picture - Why Network Marketing is Booming. (Legacy Communications, 1996)

Billac, Pete S., Sharon Davis (Editor) and Cliff Evans (Editor). The Millionaires Are Coming! How to Succeed in Network Marketing. Earn from $1,000 a Month to $1,000,000 A Year

Butwin, Robert. Street-Smart Network Marketing: A No-Nonsense Guide for Creating the Most Richly Rewarding Lifestyle You Can Possibly Imagine. (Rocklin, CA: Prima Publishing, 1997)

Christensen, Mary and Wayne Christensen. Make Your First Million in Network Marketing. (Adams Media Corporation, Due 2001)

Clements, Leonard and Corey Augenstein. The Definitive Guide to Understanding Network Marketing Compensation Plans. Available at www.upline.com.

Clements, Leonard W. Inside Network Marketing: An Expert's View into the Hidden Truths and Exploited Myths of America's Most Misunderstood Industry. (Revised and Updated 2nd Edition) (Rocklin, CA: Prima Publishing, 2000)

Clements, Leonard, Publisher. Market Wave Alert Letter. Simply one of the BEST newsletters out there!

Cook, Rod. Rod Cook's How To Start Your Network Marketing Or Internet Multi-Affiliate Company. (America's MLM Consultants, 1999)

Crisp, Robert E. Raising a Giant: A Book About Becoming a Leader in Network Marketing. (Robert Crisp Enterprises, 1998)

Daigle, Kerry. Network Your Way to Millions: (Or Less If You Don't Want to Work That Hard!) (Knowledge Products, 1997)

DeGarmo, Scott and Louis Tartaglia, MD. Heart to Heart, The Real Power of Network Marketing. (Rocklin, CA: Prima Publishing)

Duncan, Ray H. The MLM Road Map: A Step-by-Step System of Building an MLM Downline. (Double Diamond Publishing, 1999)

Dilley, Carol. The Advantages of Home-Based Businesses.

Earl, Kelton Drew. The Psychology of Network Marketing. (CallOut Publishing, 1998)

Edwards, Paul, Sarah Edwards and Walter Zooi. Home Businesses You Can Buy: The Definitive Guide to Exploring Franchises, Multi-Level Marketing, and Business Opportunities Plus: How to Avoid Scams. (Putnam Publishing Group, 1997)

Failla, Don. The Basics: How to Build a Large, Successful Multi-Level Marketing Organization.

Failla, Nancy. A Better Way to a Better Life.

----------. Financial Freedom and Prosperity.

----------. How to Be a Successful Self-Employed Woman.

Fitzpatrick, Robert L. and Joyce K. Reynolds. False Profits: Seeking Financial and Spiritual Deliverance in Multi-Level Marketing and Pyramid Schemes. (Charlotte, NC: Herald Press, 1997)

Fogg, John Milton. The Concept of "The People's Franchise." Also check out his web site at www.greatestnetworker.com. Lot's of great stuff here!

----------. The Greatest Networker in the World. (Rocklin, CA: Prima Publishing, 1997).

Forrest, Edward and Richard Mizerski (Editors). Interactive Marketing: The Future Present. (NTC Business Books, 1996)

Gabbay, Shaul M. Social Capital In The Creation of Financial Capital: The Case of Network Marketing. (Stipes Publishing, 1997)

Gage, Randy. How to Build a Multi-Level Money Machine: The Science of Network Marketing. (Miami Beach, FL: GR&DI Publications, 1998)

Gage, Randy. Randy Gage's MLM Power Weekend. (Prime Concepts Group, 2002)

----------. How to Earn at Least $100,000 Per Year in Network Marketing. From Gage Direct, 1680 Michigan Ave., Miami Beach, FL 33139, 800-432-4243.

Grimes, Kevin. Grimes & Reese. Legal Aspects of Multi-Level Marketing. 208-524-0699.

Grimes, Kevin. What to Look for and What to Look Out for in Multilevel Marketing. An audio tape set. Call Sound Concepts at 800-544-7044, or log on to www.mlmlaw.com.

Guiducci, Joan. Power Calling. (Mill Valley, CA, Tonino, 1992)

Gustwiller, Diane. Putting Together Your Lifestyle Portfolio: Get More Out of Life Than You're Getting Now With...Network Marketing. (Bottom Line Boosters, 1997). Also in related audio tape by title, The "7" Minute Sizzle.

Hedges, Burke. Networking Dynamics Audio Training Audio Training Program.

----------. Who Stole the American Dream: The Book Your Boss Doesn't Want You to Read!

----------. You Can't Steal Second with Your Foot on First! Choosing to Become Independent in a Job Dependent World. (Tampa, FL: INTI Publications, 1995)

----------. You, Inc. Discover the C.E.O. Within! (Tampa, FL: INTI Publications, 1996)

Higgins, Patrick W. The Bottom Line of Network Marketing by Audio Cassette. (Media, PA: Unlimited Horizons Training, 1999)

Higgins, Patrick W. The Future is kNOWowing Network Marketing. (Media, PA: Unlimited Horizons Training, 1996)

Hirsch, Peter L, Esq. Living With Passion: 10 Simple Secrets that Guarantee Your Success. Available at www.upline.com\buy\

Kalench, John. Being the Best You Can Be in MLM : How to Train Your Way to the Top in Multi-Level Network Marketing. (San Diego, CA: Millionaires in Motion, 1990) Available at www.miminc.com/catalog.html.

Kaeter, Margaret. The Everything Network Marketing Book: How Anyone Can Achieve Easy Success, Earn a Great Income, and Enjoy a Relaxing Lifestyle   (Adams Media Corporation, 2002)

----------. The Greatest Opportunity in the History of the World: You and the Dream of the Home-Based Business. (San Diego, CA: Millionaires in Motion, 1991) Available at www.miminc.com/catalog.html.

----------. 17 Secrets of the Master Prospectors. (San Diego, CA: Millionaires in Motion, 1994) Available at www.miminc.com/catalog.html.

Kelly, Janet. Now Its Your Turn for Success: A Training and Motivational Book Specifically Designed for the Direct Sales and Multi-Level Marketing Industries. (Crown House Publishing, 2001)

King, Charles. W. and James W. Robinson. The New Professionals: The Rise of Network Marketing As the Next Major Profession. (Roseville, CA: PRIMA SOHO, 2000)

Kishel, Gregory and Patricia Kishel. Build Your Own Network Sales Business. (New York: John Wiley & Sons, 1991)

Klaus, Michael S. and Kathie Jackson Anderson. Future Choice: Why Network Marketing May Be Your Best Career Move. (Candlelight Press, 1996)

Klaver, Kim. The Truth...What it Really Takes to Make It in Network Marketing. (Max Out Productions, 1998)

Kosch, Sandra. Kosch's Guide to Network Marketing in Canada. (Incor Enterprises, 1998)

Lant, Jeffrey L. Multi-Level Money: The Complete Guide To Generating, Closing & Working With All The People You Need To Make Real Money Every Month In Network Marketing. (Cambridge, MA: JLA Publications, 1994)

Ludbrook, Edward. The Big Picture - Why Network Marketing is Booming and What it Means to You. (Legacy Communications, 1999)

Lusbrock, Edward. The Fundamentals of Network Marketing. (Legacy Communications, 1998)

Marketing Solutions and Darleen J. Hoffman. Global Home Based Business Directory: Official Publication of the Network Marketing & Direct-Selling Industries. (Marketing Solutions, 1999)

Marks, Will (Compiler). Multi-Level Marketing : The Definitive Guide to America's Top MLM Companies. Second Edition. (Arlington, TX: Summit Publishing Group, 1996)

Masi, Anthony and Erik Masi. Dream Achievers. (Possibility Press, 2001)

Molatore, Gary. Build Your Business with New Strategies as You Learn by Doing! (Gary's Ideas, 1998)

Moore, Angela L. Building a Successful Network Marketing Company : The Systems, the Products, and the Know-How You Need to Launch or Enhance a Successful MLM Company. (Rocklin, CA: Prima Publishing, 1998)

Moore, Angela L. and Lisa H. Stringfellow. The Very Best Opportunity for Women: How to Get More Out of Life Through Network Marketing. (Prima Publishing, 2001)

Nadler, Beverly. Congratulations, You Lost Your Job. (Charlottesville, VA: MLM Publishing, 1992)

Natiuk, Robert. Your Destiny: Your Life and Work Become One. (Miami Beach, FL: Gage Research & Development Inst., 1994)

----------. The Power of Inner Marketing.

Network Action Company. Network Marketing Business Builder Action Pack. (Network Action Company, 1997)

Nichols, Rod. Successful Network Marketing for the 21st Century. (Grants Pass, OR: The Oasis Press, 1995)

Paley, Russ. Network Your Way to Millions: The Definitive Step-by-Step Guide to Wealth Through Network Marketing. (Boynton Beach, FL: Wealth Building Publications, Inc., 1999)

Paley, Russ. Russ Paley's Ultimate Guide to Network Marketing: Your Step-by-Step Guide to Wealth. (Franklin Lakes, NJ: Career Press, 2000)

Pease, Allan. Questions Are the Answers: How To Get To "Yes" in Network Marketing. (Pease International, 2002)

Pilzer, Paul Zane. God Wants You to Be Rich: How and Why Everyone Can Enjoy Material and Spiritual Wealth in Our Abundant World. (Fireside, 1997)

----------. Should You Quit Before You're Fired?

Pinnock, Tom (Reader). You Can Be Rich by Thursday: Or the Secrets of Making a Fortune in Multi-Level Marketing. (Wildstone Audio, 1998)

Poe, Richard. Wave 3: The New Era in Network Marketing. (Rocklin, CA: Prima Publishing, June 1999)

----------. The Wave 3 Way to Building Your Downline. (Rocklin, CA: Prima Publishing, 1996)

----------. Wave 4: Network Marketing in the 21st Century. (Roseville, CA: Prima Publishing,

Roller, David. How to Make Big Money in Multi Level Marketing. (Prentice Hall Trade, 1989)

Rubino, Joe, Dr. Secrets of Building a Million-Dollar Network Marketing Organization from a Guy Who's BEEN THERE DONE THAT And Shows You How You Can Do It, Too. Available at www.upline.com/buy/

Ruhe, Jan. FIRE UP!

----------. MLM Nuts $ Bolts. (JR Productions, 1997)

Schreiter, Tom. Big Al Tells All. (Houston, TX: KAAS Publishing, 1985) All Tom Schreiter titles available at http://fortunenow.com/kaascatalog.htm.

----------. How to Bulid MLM Leaders for Fun and Profit.

----------. How to Create a Recruiting Explosion. (Houston, TX: KAAS Publishing, 1986)

----------. Special Offers and Quick Start Systems.

----------. Turbo MLM. (Houston, TX: KAAS Publishing, 1988)

Scott, Gini Graham. Get Rich Through Multi-Level Selling : Build Your Own Sales And Distribution Organization. (North Vancouver, BC: International Self-Counsel Press, 1995)

Scott, Gini Graham. Strike It Rich in Personal Selling: Techniques for Success in Direct Sales, Multi-Level and Network Marketing. (iUniverse.com, 2000)

----------. Success in Multi-Level Marketing. (Prentice Hall Trade, 1991)

Shapiro, Steve. Listening for Success, How to Master the Most Important Skill of Network Marketing. (Chica Publications, 2000)

Sidak , J. Gregory, Daniel F. Spubler, Gregory J. Sidak and Daniel F. Spulber. Deregulatory Takings and the Regulatory Contract: The Competitive Transformation of Network Industries in the United States.
(Cambridge Univ. Press, 1999)

Smith, D. J. MLM Laws in All 50 States.

Snetsinger, Patrick Michael. Confessions of a Multi-Level Marketer; Networking from Your Heart. (Bellevue, WA: Palinoia Press, 1997)

Stewart, David. Network Marketing: Action Guide for Success.

----------. Network Marketing in Action.

Stills, Philip. Get A Life : How To Leave That Dead-End Job Behind And Create Your Perfect Future Today! (Charlottesville, VA : Upline Press, 1995)

Stills, Philip. Romancing Your Future. (Santa Rosa, CA: Philip Stills Business Books, 1994)

Stone, Bob. Successful Direct Marketing Methods. (NTC Business Books, 1996)

Turner, Glen W. Turner, Turner, Turner : The King of Network Marketing. (GWT & Associates, 1994)

Upline™ Resources Catalog. Quarterly catalog listing relevant books, tapes and other resources.
804-979-4427.

Varey, Richard. Relationship Marketing: Dialogue and Networks in the E-Commerce Era. (John Wiley, 2002)

Ward, Randy Joe. The Greatest Home Based Business in the World. (Prosperity Publishing, 1999)

Ward, Randy Joe. Network Marketing: The Accelerated Game of Life. (Prosperity Publishing, 1999)

Ward, Randy Joe. Winning the Greatest Game of All. (Jennings, OK: Cimarron Management Corp., 1990)

Watson, Forrest E. The Network Marketer. (Emerald Ink Pub, 2002)

Windsor, Dennis. Financially Free. (Dallas, TX: Windward Press, 1990)

----------. The Script Book.

Yarnell, Mark and Rene Reid. Power Multi-Level Marketing. (Austin, TX: MYD Publications, 1990)

Yarnell, Mark and Rene Reid. The Ultimate Tapes on MLM.

Yarnell, Mark, Rene Reid Yarnell. Your First Year in Network Marketing: Overcome Your Fears, Experience Success, and Achieve Your Dreams! (Rocklin, CA: Prima Publishing, 1998)

Yarnell, Rene Reid. The New Entrepreneurs: Making a Living—Making a Life Through Network Marketing. (Quantum Leap, 1999)

Yarnell, Mark. Your Best Year in Network Marketing. (Paper Chase Pr, 2002)

Ziglar, Zig. Network Marketing for Dummies. (Hungry Minds, 2000

Direct Mail/Mail Order

Direct mail is different than other types of advertising because it is extremely targeted. When you advertise with direct mail, you are sending your offer out to people who are already likely to be interested in what you have to offer. In other words: Direct mail involves sending your information direct to your prospective clients.

It should be information that will elicit a response and/or will put you in a good position to follow up with prospects and turn them into customers. It allows you to talk directly to the most valuable people to you. If media advertising is the shotgun approach, then direct mail is the rifle - allowing you to directly address your target market with precision.

The communication can be for any of the following reasons:

- To tell prospective customers about your business
- To tell current customers about a special offer or promotion
- To remind lapsed customers about your business and maybe make them a special

Compared with other advertising vehicles, direct mail can be an economical way to reach former, current and prospective customers. But, like any marketing method, it still can be expensive. The cost depends on the choices you make in administering your direct mail campaign. 'Campaign?' you are asking. 'Isn't this just getting the word out about my business? Who said anything about a campaign?'

The fact is, whatever type of marketing tools you employ, it is crucial to think of your efforts as a coordinated program. Doing that will force you to think carefully about what you are saying in all your efforts. And careful, coordinated planning will help you develop a consistent message that people will remember.

It has been proven that over 50% of Direct Mail recipients read it immediately and of those, over 40% found the information useful. Studies have shown that every dollar spent on Direct Mail advertising brings in $10 in sales.

List Selection

Knowing your audience is crucial. This means starting with a list of current and former customers, identifying their common characteristics and using that information as a road map for identifying potential new customers as well. Common factors can include geographic location, profession, even consumer trends. If you do a lot of business with architects, space planners or interior designers, for example, remember that there are specialties within those disciplines, and target your direct mail marketing program to the specialties which

As a result, the quality of the mailing list that you use is vital for the success of your direct mail campaign. Ideally the list must contain all of your defined target audience, and no more.

- Your direct mail list should be highly configurable. This will enable you to tailor the list to your ideal target market.

- Your direct mail list should contain contact names as well as job titles. Addressing your target as "The Marketing Manager" will never yield as good a result as "Dear Mrs Roberts" or "Dear Jane". A list without a name makes your letter look like it is part of a bulk direct mail shot people respond best to letters sent especially to them (even if that is only an illusion).

- Your direct mail list must be updated frequently. People move jobs and getting the name wrong is arguable even worse than not having a name at all.

Yes, you do have the beginnings of your own direct mail list. It may be on the back of old receipts or in a guest register, or simply in your reservations book, but it exists. You can add to this list by finding potential customers. Approach your local Chamber of Commerce, or the tourist board. They will have some databases available to you if you are a member for a nominal fee. Collect all your names and addresses on a simple computer database so you can print off labels. A typed label will help ensure that your mail arrives and has a professional edge. Make sure all addresses are complete. That means: full title and surname, house number or name, street, town or city and, above all, the postcode. There is no point in sending a piece of

Before You Start

Before writing a direct mail piece, you will need to answer some basic questions:

- What do you wish to achieve?
- How are you going to achieve this?
- How will you want people to respond?
- What are your strengths over the competition?
- What is the current situation in your area e.g. are there any other special offers that you are aware of that will have an effect on your campaign?
- Do you have a unique selling proposition?
- What can you offer these people that will entice them to

Checking Your Sales Letter (Copy)

Take time to craft a suitable offer that will appeal to your target market. The key is to ensure that you tell your reader quickly in the text what you are offering him and that it is appropriate to him. You could say: "The Seagull Restaurant would like to welcome you back to dine with 20% discount." Make sure your offer is simple, of good value and relevant to your target market.

The effectiveness of your direct mail message rests largely on your ability to put yourself in your prospect's place and answer this question, 'What does a prospect need to know about my capabilities if I am to improve my chances of getting my foot in the door?'

Good sales letters have:
A headline that is a bold statement, catching the eye of the potential client:
For example:
"*Why pay more tax than you need to*"
"*Low Risks with High Returns*"

Then short, basic wording explaining:

- Who you are
- What your offer is
- Why you are different
- What the benefits are

Answer potential questions about the offer in your communication. And most importantly make it easy for them to respond, giving your telephone number and reinforcing the offer or message in your final paragraph.

And finally, EVERY mailer should have several ways of getting in touch with you. Sending out good information with poor contact information is simply a waste of money.

The Advantages of Direct Mail

- You can pinpoint your target audience, so waste is kept to a minimum.
- You have measurable results and can calculate your cost-per-order or cost-per-response.
- Direct Mail can drive sales and build awareness to your company or product which results in a win-win situation.
- You can mail the amount, type and message of your choice.
- You choose the audience you want to target.
- Your message goes straight to your customer without

Using Direct Mail to Create Income

Direct mail can be used to enhance your own small business, promote your website, or sell any of your products you have put into your funnel.

Let's go through this as an instructive example. Let's say you have access to 2 groups: The North American High School Teacher's Association and High School Teachers Today. How big are the lists? One of them is about 3,800, and the other one is about 4,500.

After checking the two databases, you find that you have 3000 unique and full addresses. You now need to send these 3000 potential consumers a postcard. Postage per postcard is 21 cents and the entire mailing with postage and all will cost you about 30 cents a piece. Now remember, to get the twenty-one cent rate on the postcard, it's got to be a small postcard. There is a certain height and length requirement and if you go over it, you will get all of your postcards back!! Keeping to the smaller sized postcard, this entire mailing will cost you $900.

The main thing you are looking for are email addresses. How do you get email addresses via mail? You seduce them to go to a web page and make them an offer for an inexpensive front-end product. If they don't buy it, there will be a pop-up menu that says, "Wait a second! Don't leave yet! Sign up for High School Teachers free tips!" In this way, you will capture their email and from then on, you will be able to use targeted email via your auto responder to pull them into your funnel.

Let's look at this carefully. If your product is $30.00 digital product, how many people do you need to break even? You need 30 people to order the product. You would also like to get two or three hundred people to sign up for the free tips.

New customers can be sold low-end products only. With existing customers who have already purchased from you, however, it is possible to get them to buy higher end products just from a postcard. For example, past customer's may come to your seminar as a result of a postcard mailer, even though it's a $97 product.

When you do postcard mailings, make them wild, bright, neon colors such as fuchsia, green, or yellow. You want to get their attention. Once you get people into your funnel, cha-ching, you are on your way to residual income.

Postcards are the only method of traditional direct marketing that's still affordable because postcards are inexpensive to mail. The beauty about a postcard is that you can direct them to a pre-recorded message or send them to an e-mail address. Additionally, when they arrive at the door, they are already opened. Your prospective customer doesn't have to open an envelope.

Remember, your goal with prospects is to get them to take one specific action. You want them to either call or fax or send an email. You don't have a lot of room on a postcard, so don't try to do more than get them to take a specific action.

For example, if I was doing a pitch for an event, I would say "If you're interested in marketing information products, you need to find out about how to blah blah blah blah blah and get filthy rich, go to this link." And, so they go to the link and it would be a description of a seminar, a very lengthy description, trying to get them to sign up for the seminar.

Let's go through this as an instructive example. In this instance, I will be sending out 3000 cards. Postage per postcard is 21 cents and the entire mailing with postage and all will cost me about 30 cents a piece, or $900. The purpose of this postcard is two-fold: capturing email addresses and breaking even on the front end (this keeps me from wasting cash flow.) So, the postcard will seduce them to go to a web page where I will make them an offer for an inexpensive front-end product. If they don't buy it, there will be a pop-up menu that says, "Wait a second! Don't leave yet! Sign up for Jim's free tips!" So, if I can't get them on the front-end product, I'll try to capture at least

If my product is $30.00 digital product, how many people do I need to break even? I need 30 people to order the product. With this post card, I want to get at least 30 people to buy my digital product and get at least two or three hundred people to sign up for the free tips. Once I get these people into my funnel, I'll begin sending them auto responder messages to get them to buy other products.

Bibliography:

Arnold, Peter. Making Direct Mail Work for You: Get Great Results from All Your Direct Mail. (How to Books, 2001)

Atwood, Tony. Raising Response Rate in Direct Mail. (First and Best in Education, LTD, 2002)

Baird, L. Lawrence. Mail Order Millions: It Worked for Me...It Will Work for You. (Baird-Hedges Publishing, 1995)

Benson, Richard V. Secrets of Successful Direct Mail. (Passport Books, 1991)

Blum, Sandra J. Designing Direct Mail That Sells. (Northlight Books, 1999)

Bly, Robert W. The Copywriter's Handbook: A Step-By-Step Guide to Writing Copy That Sells. (Henry Holt, 1990)

Bly, Robert W. Business to Business Direct Marketing: Proven Direct Response Methods to Generate More Leads and Sales. (NTC Business Books, 1998)

Bly, Robert W. The Encyclopedia of Business Letters, Fax Memos, and E-Mail. (Career Press, 1999)

Bly, Robert W. The Perfect Sales Piece: A Complete Do-It-Yourself Guide to Creating Brochures, Catalogs, Fliers, and Pamphlets. (New York: John Wiley & Sons, 1994)

Bly, Robert W. Power-Packed Direct Mail: How to Get More Leads and Sales by Mail. (Henry Holt, 1995)

Bly, Robert W. Start and Run a Profitable Mail-Order Business. (Self Counsel Press, 1994)

Bodian, Nat G. Direct Marketing Rules of Thumb: 1,000 Practical and Profitable Ideas to Help You Improve Response, Save Money, and Increase Efficiency in Your Direct Program. (New York: McGraw-Hill, 1995)

Bolden, Tanya. Mail Order and Direct Response. (Borders Press, 1994)

Bond, William J. Home-Based Catalog Marketing: A Success Guide for Entrepreneurs. (New York: McGraw-Hill, 1993)

Burstiner, Irving. Mail Order Selling: How to Market Almost Anything by Mail. (New York: John Wiley & Sons, 1995)

Cohen, William A. Building a Mail Order Business: A Complete Manual for Success. (New York: John Wiley & Sons, 1996)

Cossman, E. Joseph. How I Made $1,000,000 in Mail Order. (Fireside, 1993)

Edwards, Paul and Sarah Edwards. Getting Business to Come to You: Everything You Need to Do Your Own Advertising, Public Relations, Direct Mail and Sales Promotions and Attract All the Business You Can Handle. (Putnam Publishing Group, 1991)

Effron, Gil. Direct Mail Success. (Glenn Bridge Press, 2000)

Fairlie, Robin. Database Marketing and Direct Mail. (Kogan Page, 1993)

Ferdi, Liz. Successful Direct Mail. (Barron's Educational Series, 1991)

Fiumara, Georganne. How to Start a Home-Based Mail-Order Business. (Globe Pequot Press, 1999)

Geller, Lois K. Direct Marketing Techniques: Building Your Business Using Direct Mail and Direct Response Advertising. (Crisp Publications, 1998)

Grensing, Lin. A Small Business Guide to Direct Mail: Build Your Customer Base and Boost Profits. (Self Counsel Press, 1991)

Griffith, Roger M. What a Way to Live and Make a Living: The Lyman P. Wood Story. (In Brief Press, 1994)

Hahn, Fred E. Do-It-Yourself Advertising & Promotion: How to Produce Great Ads, Brochures, Catalogs, Direct Mail, and Much More. (New York: John Wiley & Sons, 1997)

Hatch, Denny. Million Dollar Mailing$. (Bonus Books, 2001)

Hicks, Tyler G. 101 Great Mail-Order Businesses: The Very Best (And Most Profitable!) Mail-Order Businesses You Can Start With Little Or No Money. (Rocklin, CA: Prima Pub., 2000)

Hicks, Tyler G. How I Grossed More Than One Million Dollars in Direct Mail & Mail Order Starting With Little Cash & Less Know-How. (International Wealth Success, 1993)

Hicks, Tyler G. Mail Order Success Secrets: How To Create a $1,000,000-A-Year Business Starting From Scratch. (Rocklin, CA: Prima Publ., 1998)

Jefkins, Frank William. Sell Anything by Mail! (Adams Media Corporation, 1990)

Joffe, Gerardo. How You Too Can Make At Least $1 Million (But Probably Much More) In The Mail-Order Business. (North Vancouver, BC: Self-Counsel Press, 1992)

Johnson, Deborah and Steve Kennedy. How to Farm Successfully--By Mail: A Complete Guide for Real Estate Professionals. (Argyle Press, 1995)

Keup, Erwin J. Mail Order Legal Guide. (Oasis Press, 1993)

Kern, Russell M. S.U.R.E.-Fire Direct Response Marketing : Managing Business-to-Business Sales Leads for Bottom-Line Success. (McGraw-Hill Trade, 2001)

Kobliski, Kathy J. Advertising Without an Agency: A Comprehensive Guide to Radio, Television, Print, Direct Mail, and Outdoor Advertising for Small Business. (PSI Research-Oasis Press, 1998)

Kremer, John. Mail Order Selling Made Easier: How to Plan, Organize, and Carry out a Successful Direct Mail Promotion. (Open Horizons Publishing, 1989)

Lewis, Hershcell Gordon. Open Me Now. (Bonus Books, 1995)

Lister, Gwyneth J. Building Your Direct Mail Program. (Jossey-Bass, 2001)

MacPherson, Kim. Permission-Based E-Mail Marketing That Works. (Dearborn Trade, 2001)

Maitland, Iain. How to Plan Direct Mail. (Cassell Academic, 1997)

Mallory, Charles. Direct Mail Magic. (1991, ISBN: 1560520752)

Masser, Barry Z. How to Make 100,000 a Year in Home Mail Order Business. (Prentice Hall Press, 1992)

McElhone, Alice Powers and Edward B. Butler. Mail It! High-Impact Business Mail from Design to Delivery. Benchmark Publications, 1996)

Muldoon, Katie. How To Profit Through Catalog Marketing. (Lincolnwood, IL: NTC Business Books, 1996)

Nicholas, Ted. The Golden Mailbox: How to Get Rich Direct Marketing Your Product. (Dearborn Financial Publishing, 1992)

Padgett, JoAnn (Editor). Start Your Own Mail Order Business. (San Diego, CA: Pfeiffer & Co., 1994)

Pearson, Stewart. Building Brands Directly: Creating Business Value from Customer Relationships. (New York University Press, 1995)

Primm, Roy. 257 Ways to Avoid Wasting Money in Mail Order-And Grow Richer! (Roy J. Primm Research, 1990)

Print Project. Wholesale By Mail And Online 2000. (New York: HarperResource, 1999)

Roberts, Stevan, Michelle Feit and Robert W. Bly. Internet Direct Mail: The Complete Guide to Successful E-Mail Marketing Campaigns. (NTC Business Books, 2000)

Robinson, John Fraser. Effective Direct Mail. (David Grant, 2000)

Sackheim, Maxwell. Max Sackheim's Billion Dollar Marketing Concepts and Applications: The Man Who Revolutionized 20th Century Direct Response Advertising. (TOWERS Club, 1996)

Schmid, Jack. Creating a Profitable Catalog: Everything You Need to Know to Create a Catalog That Sells. (NTC/Contemporary Publishing, 2000)

Schultz, Marilyn Smith. Mail Order on the Kitchen Table. (Tribute, 1989)

Simon, Julian Lincoln. How To Start And Operate A Mail-Order Business. (New York: McGraw-Hill, 1993)

Sugarman, Joseph. Marketing Secrets of a Mail Order Maverick: Stories & Lessons on the Power of Direct Marketing to Start a Successful Business, Create a Famous Brand. (Delstar Publishing, 1998)

Tedesco, T. J. (Editor). Direct Mail Pal: A Direct Mail Production Handbook. (Graphic Arts Techical Foundation, 2002)

Thomas, Brian. Royal Mail Guide to Direct Mail for Small Businesses. (Butterworth-Heinemann, 1997)

Throckmorton, Jaon and Thomas L. Collins. Winning Direct Response Advertising: From Print Through Interactive Media. (NTC Business Books, 1997)

Vernon, Lillian. An Eye for Winners: How I Built One of America's Greatest Direct-Mail Business. (HarperCollins, 1997)

Warwick, Mal. 999 Tips, Trends, and Guidelines for Successful Direct Mail and Telephone Fundraising. (Strathmoor Press, 1995)

Warwick, Mal. Testing, Testing, 1,2,3,: Raise More Money with Direct Mail Tests. (Jossey Bass, 2003)

White, Sarah. Streetwise Do-It-Yourself Advertising: Create Great Ads, Promotions, Direct Mail, and Marketing Strategies That Will Send Your Sales Soaring) (Adams Media Corporation, 1997)

Wilbur, L. Perry. How to Make Money in Mail-Order. (New York: John Wiley & Sons, 1990)

Wilbur, L. Perry. Money in Your Mailbox: How to Start and Operate a Successful Mail-Order Business. (New York: John Wiley & Sons, 1993)

Franchising

Almost 50% of all retail sales in the United States are controlled by franchises, from grocery stores, to car repair shops to delivery companies, franchises is everywhere. So, what is franchising? Franchising is one of three business strategies a company may use in capturing market share. The others are company owned units or a combination of company owned and franchised units.

Franchising is a business strategy for getting and keeping customers. It is a marketing system for creating an image in the minds of current and future customers about how the company's products and services can help them. It is a method for distributing products and services that satisfy customer needs.

Franchising is a network of interdependent business relationships that allows a number of people to share:

- A brand identification
- A successful method of doing business
- A proven marketing and distribution system

In short, franchising is a strategic alliance between groups of people who have specific relationships and responsibilities with a common goal to dominate markets, i.e., to get and keep more customers than their competitors. Other franchisees and company-operated units are not your competition. The opposite is true. They and you share the task of establishing the brand as the dominant brand in all markets entered and reinforcing the customers' familiarity with and trust in the brand. So in this respect you are working as a team with others in the system. Other franchisees share with you the responsibility for quality, consistency, convenience, and other factors that define your franchise and insures repeat business for everyone. Increasing the value of the

The History of Franchising

Franchising finds its roots before the Middle Ages. It first appeared commercially in the United States before the Civil War, likely with Robert Fulton and his licensing of his steamboats and emerged as a force to be reckoned with in the post World War II 1950's. It boomed in the 60's. It policed itself in the 70's and it matured in the 80's and

90's. Franchising has become one of the most dominant forces in the world economy today.

According to every government survey, franchising has experienced explosive growth since the mid-70s and is expected to be the leading method of doing business in the new century. In the United States, there are over 2,500 franchise systems. These systems have in excess of 534,000 franchise units, which represent 3.2% of the total businesses. This 3.2% of all businesses controls over 35% of all retail and service revenue in the U.S. economy.

Types of Franchises

Many people are not aware that there are two types of franchises:

- Product / Tradename Franchises
- Business Format Franchises

In Product / Tradename Franchises, the franchisee has use of a product or trade name but has no supporting relationship with franchisor. This means that the franchisee basically operates the business independently but the franchisee does benefit from the marketing and advertising efforts of the franchise system.
The products that are franchised are generally the older, established ones with a proven customer base. The most common product and trade name franchises are auto dealerships, gas stations, and soft-

The Business Format Franchise is faster growing and is the format most people are interested in today. It is characterized by an ongoing business relationship between franchisor and franchisee. The franchisee is offered not only a trademark and logo but also a complete operational system. Business format franchises are famous throughout the world with participants such as McDonald's, Holiday Inn, Midas, Century 21 and Baskin-Robbins, to name a few.

In the best of all worlds, the business format franchise is mutually beneficial, for both the franchisor and the franchisee. The franchisee, by paying an initial fee and, often, an ongoing royalty fee, gives the franchise system a continuous supply of working capital to develop and expand the organization. In turn, the franchisee gets a business package that would take years to develop and refine. This gives the franchisee a strengthened ability to compete through the established brand identity and marketing power of the system, and the cost benefits and clout of the franchisor's collective purchasing power.

Advantages of Franchise Ownership

The benefits of franchise ownership are only as strong as the franchise you select. Generally speaking, the benefits can be classified in several broad areas:

1. **Overall Competitive Benefits**: The public has become accustom to a certain level of quality and consistency from brand name franchised locations. Whether you believe a company's product is superior or mediocre, the secret for their success is usually that it is consistent. The consumer knows the level of quality they will receive in every location they visit. This brand identification often provides the new franchisee with an established customer base accustomed to shopping under the company's brand and that makes it easier to compete with the well-established independent operators and even against other

2. **Pre-Opening Benefits**: Franchisors have made mistakes. Another advantage of franchising is that they have survived their mistakes and can guide their franchisees not to make the same mistakes. Upon joining an established franchise system new franchisees generally receive comprehensive initial training in the operating of the franchise system, its product, services and methodologies. While the cost of entrance into a franchise system includes a franchise fee - often cited as a disadvantage - the franchisee benefits from a host of services including operations manuals, site selection, store design, construction programs and reduced cost of equipment to name just a few. Additionally, they have not only their franchisor as a seasoned partner to ask questions to but the network of other franchisees

    In essence, the major stumbling block for pre-destined failure is removed by the franchisor - lack of preparedness. Most independent businesses don't fail because their product or services were inadequate. They fail because they did not anticipate problems. Chief among these is working capital. Well-developed franchise programs ensure that before they accept a new franchisee that they have adequate capital, even after servicing their debt and taking into account seasonally adjusted cash flow. Without this guidance many independent operators fail soon after opening.

3. **Ongoing Benefits**: In exchange for paying an ongoing royalty and other payments, franchisees generally receive continual training programs and other ongoing home office and field support and assistance.

Group purchasing power is a major benefit of well-developed franchise systems. Frequently buying groups established by the franchisor allow the franchisees to benefit from a lower cost of goods, equipment, and supplies than that available to independent operators.

Leveraging off the contributions of the entire franchise system, franchisors are able to create professionally designed point of sale, advertising, grand opening programs and other marketing materials that independents could never afford. Franchise programs can also afford to continue to modernize the system through ongoing research and development and the test marketing of new products and operating programs.

Franchising is a critical mass business both with a market and system wide. The spending power of the individual dollar, combined with their fellow franchisees within their market and the rest of the system enable franchises not only to dominate local markets and established independents but also to compete effectively against the established large chains.

Buying a Franchise

There are many misconceptions about franchising, but probably the most widely held is that you as a franchisee are "buying a franchise." In reality you are investing your assets in a system to utilize the brand name, operating system and ongoing support. You and everyone in the system are licensed to use the brand name and operating system.

Why is it a lease? In any franchise deal the franchisee receives the assets upfront but only for a limited period of time--the term of the franchise agreement. The term of the agreement may run 5 or 10 years or, in some cases, only 1 or 2 years. At the end of the term, the franchisor decides whether or not the agreement will be renewed. The reasons for not renewing the agreement should be completely spelled out in the Uniform Franchise Offering Circular and franchise agreement.

An "ownership mentality" destroys the reason franchised and company-operated units are successful. Think about it. If you think you "bought" a franchise, you become an "owner" and begin to think and act like an owner. You will want to change the system because of your needs, you will wonder what you are paying the royalty for, and you will begin thinking of other franchisees as your competitors. For these and many other reasons you do not want to think of yourself as an "independent owner."

Steps to Acquiring a Franchise

Step 1: First, you must determine if you would function well as a franchisee.

Your job is to make an informed business decision about whether a franchisor's business opportunity meets your needs and whether you can provide what the franchisor wants and needs in a franchisee.

You need to ask yourself basic questions:

1. What do you want from life at this time?

2. What are your wants, needs, and desires?

3. What are your goals, objectives, and dreams?

4. What are you looking for in a business?

5. Have you decided to leave what you are now doing–not just the job, but the profession?

6. Have you made a decision to become a part of another organization? Remember that in franchising you joined someone else's business. You are going to be using their marketing system to generate customers and their operating system to satisfy them.

7. Do you have the kind of personality that can accept running the business according to someone else's plan without feeling that it compromises your individuality?

8. Do you have an interest in doing this kind of work for the length of the agreement?

9. Have you ever worked for one company for five or ten years?

10. Do you have related skills, knowledge, abilities, and work-related experiences similar to the ones required for running the franchise you are considering?

11. Do you have the financial resources to open and operate the business successfully?

12. Can the business support your lifestyle needs?

13. Which of the franchises you are reviewing meets your financial needs short and long term?

Step 2: You then have to choose the right franchise among the 3000-plus franchise selections available. Most franchisor's today have web pages with tons of information on their companies and their franchise opportunities. Evaluate the legal documents from a business perspective. Determine whether the franchisor has territory policies that might make franchisees less competitive in a highly competitive environment. Many prospective franchisees erroneously believe that having a large territory is best for them. It could, in fact, be the worst thing for them. For example, if you have too few franchisees in a market and competitors have more units than you have, it could leave you at a disadvantage in terms of dominating the market for your

Look for a franchisor who can communicate a strategy not just for market presence but for dominating markets; look for a franchisor interested in establishing a competitive edge and increasing market share. If a franchisor cannot talk about these issues, it is entirely possible the franchisor is using franchising as a way to generate franchise fees and royalty revenue rather than to establish a competitive position in the marketplace.

Evaluate the marketing/advertising fee. Many franchisors and prospective franchisees erroneously believe that a low marketing fee is a good thing. In fact, the marketing fee should be related to the amount of money each franchisee needs to contribute to support an advertising campaign that will generate enough new and repeat business for each of them. A 1% advertising fee may look good now, but when you need 5% from everyone to be competitive, it might not be possible to convince all franchisees to participate.

Evaluate the effectiveness of the Franchise Advisory Council. Does the franchisor incorporate the franchisees' input in the decisions that affect the future direction of the system? Does the franchisor involve franchisees' input in decisions?

Be sure you can answer the question "How will I make money in this business?" There should be a very simple answer to this question. It will not violate earnings claims restrictions for the franchisor to answer it because you are not asking "How much money will I make?" You simply want to know how money is made in the business. Spend as much time as possible speaking to existing franchisees. Ask them if they would do it again. How long did it take them to recoup their investment? How much money are they making? Does the operating system work? Are they provided with good marketing programs? Do the franchisees get along well with each other and with the franchisor? What are the major problems with the business? Do they use all of the operating system? Is the franchisor's ongoing support adequate and helpful? The answers to these questions will help you make your

Step 3: After you narrow down your franchise choices, you must then thoroughly investigate each opportunity.

After your preliminary research, you're going to contact the franchise systems you're interested in. You will receive an information package from each company. By the way, this is a good way for you to begin to evaluate the franchise. You might want to think over whether or not you want to pursue this particular opportunity if it takes a month or more to receive the information or if you can't even get to this point because all you do is leave voice mail messages for the franchise development department.

Generally, a franchise information package will contain a letter, a brochure describing the business and a qualifying questionnaire. The questionnaire usually asks for the following information:

- Assets
- Liabilities
- Net Worth
- Sources of Income
- Educational History

- Previous Employment
- Credit References
- Personal References
- Motivation for Buying a Franchise

The franchisor should have a business plan for the system that covers at least the length of the agreement you are being asked to commit to. Ask for the plan for the market where you are going to locate the operation. Ask for their analysis of the competition. Ask how many units are being planned for your area and why that many. Why not more, why not less? Ask how much is going to be spent on marketing in your area.

Ask to look at the operations manuals or at least to see an outline of them. This is important because the operations manuals are your guideline to a successful operation. You need to feel comfortable that they are complete and clear and meet your abilities, needs, and goals.

Ask to receive a full explanation of the initial and subsequent training programs. Ask how people are trained. Is it classroom or hands-on practice? Are there case studies and discussions or is it straight lecture?

Ask for a full explanation of the pre-opening assistance offered by the franchisor. Understand any help franchisors give for site selection and lease negotiation. Be clear about what ongoing support the franchisor provides to the franchisees.

Step 4: Once you have made a choice you must analyze and understand the franchise agreement and, if possible, negotiate points of disagreement with the franchisor. The disclosure document will provide you with a wealth of information that you should have reviewed by your accountant as well as a qualified franchise attorney. Many prospective franchisees unfortunately rely upon their local lawyers for advice on franchising matters. Franchising is a complicated and somewhat unique branch of the law and requires you to work with lawyers that practice in this area. A good source for locating a qualified franchise attorney is through the International Franchise Association at

Step 5: Finally, you will have to put together a financial package to fund your franchise investment.

Creating Your Own Franchise

Picture this: a terrier, smartly dressed in a red bandanna; a German shepherd wearing a police badge; and a springer spaniel, lovingly held by its owner. These are some of the clients Bill and Peggy Cain snap in their Bow, New Hampshire, portrait studio.

When Bill started his photography business 12 years ago, he noticed many customers wanted their pets included in family portraits. That gave him the idea for Dog Gone Portraits, a portrait studio for man's best friend and other critters. The Cains' studio averages some 1,000 sittings each year.

The Cains have just begun franchising their concept. Start-up costs of $22,400 to $36,000 cover the $15,000 franchise fee, equipment and training. The Cains run their studio from home, and franchisees can do the same by working with pet stores and pet-related associations that sponsor on-site photo programs in return for a percentage of sales. A photography background is helpful but not necessary; training involves photography lessons and tips on posing the furry subjects.

You need to look at your business and imagine that you're actively engaged in the process of readying it for franchise. That you are ready to create 5,000 businesses exactly like it. If you can think about your business in this way, if you can imagine what kind of systems, what kind of checks and balances you would need to achieve this result, then you can see what you have to do. You can see your mission clearly.

Every franchise in operation has done this to varying degrees. McDonald's, Starbucks, RadioShack, Baskin-Robbins...the list goes on and on. Don't let the magnitude of these corporations alienate you from the fundamental reality--that these companies employ techniques and strategies that are accessible to ALL business owners...even you!

It's not that they have exceptional products or services. They have exceptional businesses...their business model is their single most important product. If no aspect of a business is left to chance, the owner or operator's ability to achieve their business and life goals is greatly enhanced! The owner or operator's ability to remove themselves from the daily operating reality of the business becomes possible!

Here are four things to consider when gearing up to create your franchise prototype. They are the governing rules in the franchise game, and will provide you with a context in which to look at your business as a franchise prototype.
Your business will:
- Provide consistent value to your customers, employees, suppliers, and lenders, and will exceed their expectations
- Be positioned to be operated by people with the lowest possible level of skill, because everything in the business will be systematized
- Be the exemplar of order, and will provide a predictable experience for your customers, employees, suppliers, and lenders
- Have all the work that happens documented in an Operations

Creating the manuals, systems, formats, etc, will take time, money, and effort. Once these are established, however, you can begin selling your franchise like Dog Gone Portraits did. Let's say that you sell 3 franchises per year at a profit of $15,000. That is an extra $45,000 to invest, creating even more residual income.

Bibliography:

Alon, Ilon. The Internationalization of United States Franchizing Systems. (Garland Publishing, 1999)

Arden, Lynie. Franchises You Can Run From Your Home. (John, Wiley, and Sons, 1990)

Arden, Lynie, Constance Jones and Philip Lie. 220 Best Franchises to Buy: The Essential Sourcebook for Evaluating the Best Franchise Opportunities. (Broadway Books, 2000)

American Bar Association. Building Franchise Relationships: A Guide to Anticipating Problems, Resolving Conflicts, and Representing. (American Bar Association, 1996)

American Bar Association. Franchise Protection : Laws Against Termination and the Establishment of Additional Franchises. (American Bar Association, 1990)

American Bar Association. Franchise Trademark Handbook: Developing and Protecting Your Trademarks and Service Marks. (American Bar Association, 1994)

Attwood, Tony and Len Hough. The Good Franchise Guide. (Beekman Publishing , 1989)

Aubry, M. C. Franchise Your Way To Wealth: How To Expand A Business--Yours Or Someone Else's--Into A Franchise Fortune. (Aubry Corp., 1993)

Banning, Kent B. Opportunities in Franchising Careers. (Lincolnwood, IL: VGM Career Horizons, 1996)

Barrow, Colin and Godfrey Golzen. Taking Up a Franchise. (Beekman Publishing, 1991)

Birkeland, Peter M. Franchising Dreams: The Lure of Entrepreneurship in America. (University of Chicago Press, 2002)

Bond, Robert E. Bond's Franchise Guide 2001. (Source Book Publications, 2001)

Bond, Robert E. Bond's Minority Franchise Guide: 2000. (Source Book Publications, 2001)

Bond, Robert. Bond's Top 50 New Franchises. (Sobo Visual Arts, 1999)

Bond, Robert. Bond's Top 50 Retail Franchises. (Sobo Visual Arts, 1999)

Bond, Robert, Steve Schiller and Nicole Thompson. Bond's Top 50 Service-Based Franchises. (Source Book Publications, 2000)

Bond, Robert and Nicole Thompson. Bond's Top Fifty Food Service Franchises. (Source Book Publications, 2000)

Bond, Robert. E. The Franchise Yearbook 2000. (Source Book Publications, 2001)

Bond, Robert E. "How Much Can I Make?: Actual Sales And Profit Potential For Your Small Business. 9Oakland, CA: Source Book Publications, 1997)

Bond, Robert. Bond's Top 100 Franchises: An In Depth Analysis of Today's Top Franchise Opportunities. (Source Book Pubns, 2002)

Boroian, Donald D. and Patrick J. Boroian. The Franchise Advantage: Make It Work for You. (Chicago Review Press, ISBN: 0931073030)

Bradach, Jeffrey L. and Harvard Business School Press. Franchise Organizations. (New York: McGraw-Hill, 1998, 2000)

Butler, Walter. How To Win The Franchise And Influence People. (Visionwise, Ltd., ISBN 0946572003)

Cameron, Jan. The Franchise Handbook; A Complete Guide To Selecting, Buying, And Operating. (Barnes & Noble, ISBN: 0389003344)

Carlyle, Christopher Company. Entrepreneur's Guide to Buying a Small Business Franchise or Non-Franchise. (Carlyle Publishing, 1997)

Clarke, Greg. Buying Your First Franchise. (Kogan Page, 1996)

Coltman, Michael M. Franchising in Canada: Pros and Cons. (Self-Counsel Press, 1997)

Coltman, Michael M. Franchising in the U.S.: Pros and Cons. (Self-Counsel Press, 1990)

Dixon, Ted. The 2001 Franchise Annual. (Info Press, 2001)

Dugan, Anne and The Association of Small Business Development. Franchising 101: The Complete Guide to Evaluating, Buying and Growing Your Franchised Business. (Upstart Publishing, 1998)

Edwards, Paul, Sarah Edwards and Walter Zooi. Home Businesses You Can Buy: The Definitive Guide to Exploring Franchises, Multi-Level Marketing, and Business Opportunities Plus: How to Avoid Scams. (Putnam Publishing Group, 1997)

Evaluating a Franchise. (International Specialized Book Services, 1995)

Felstead, Alan. The Corporate Paradox: Power and Control in the Business Franchise. (International Thomson Publishers, 1994)

Fern, Martin. Establishing and Operating under a Franchise Relationship. (Matthew Bender & Co., ISBN: 0820524042)

Finn, Richard. Your Fortune in Franchise. (Chicago: Contemporary Books, 1979)

Foltz, Donald J. College of Franchise Knowledge: What You Should Know About Choosing and Buying a Franchise. (Franchise Center, 1992)

Foster, Donald J. The Complete Franchise Book: Everything You Need to Know about Buying or Starting Your Own Franchise. (Prima Communications, 1993)

Foster, Dennis L. The Complete Franchise Book: What You Must Know (And Are Rarely Told) About Buying Or Starting Your Own Franchise. (Prima Publishing, ISBN: 0914629247)

Foster, Dennis L. Franchising for Free: Owning Your Own Business without Investing Your Own Cash. (New York: John Wiley & Sons, 1988)

Fox, Steven A. Franklin J. Plewa and George Friedlob. Keys to Buying a Franchise (Barron's Educational Series, 1991)

Franchise and Business Opportunities Directory (21st Edition) (Franchise & Business Opportunities, 2001)

Frisch, Carlienne A. Careers in Starting and Building Franchises. (Rosen Publishing Group, 1998)

Green, Carol B. The Franchise Survival Guide: Real-World Solutions for Turning Your Investment into a Money-Making Business. (New York: McGraw-Hill, 1993)

Griser, William A. Franchise and Business Opportunities: Executive Edition for the Entrepreneur. (Franchise Business Opportunities Publishing Co., ISBN: 0964588617)

Griser, William A. Franchise and Business Opportunities: The Key to Independence, Economic Growth and Stability. (Franchise & Business Opportunities Publishing Company, 2000)

Heckman, Lucy. Franchising in Business: A Guide to Information Sources. (Garland Publishing, 1989)

Hicks, Tyler G. Franchise Riches Success Kit. (International Wealth Success, 1992)

Hjelmfelt, David C. Understanding Franchise Contracts. (Pilot Books, ISBN: 0875761100)

International Franchise Association. Franchise Opportunities Guide: Fall Winter 1998. (International Franchise Association, 1998)

Keup, Irwin J. Franchise Bible: How to Buy a Franchise or Franchise Your Own Business. (PSI Research, 2000)

Khan, Mahmood A. Restaurant Franchising. (New York: John Wiley & Sons, 1999)

Koppell, G. Oliver. What to Consider Before Buying a Franchise. (Albany, NY: New York State Department of Law, 1994)

Kranendonk, Barbara. Married and Making a Living: Who Own Small Franchise Businesses. (Garland Publishing, 1998)

Lasher, William. Small-Business Franchise Made Simple. (New York: Doubleday, 1994)

Lewis Warren L. Franchises Dollar$ & Sense: A Guide Couples For Evaluating Franchises And Potential Franchise Earnings. (Kendall/Hunt, 1993)

Lewis, Mack O. How to Franchise Your Business: A Quick Step-By-Step Guide. (Pilot Books, ISBN: 087576147X)

Leibowitz, Martin L., Stanley Kogelman and John W. Peavey. Franchise Value and the Price/Earnings Ratio. (Research Foundation of ICFA, 2000)

Liebowitz, Martin L. and Keith C. Brown. Sales-Driven Franchise Value. (Association for Investment, 2000)

Limulus, Inc. Staff. Fast Food and Quick Service Restaurant Franchises: The North American Directory. (Limulus, Inc., 1994)

Lockerby, Michael J. Trade Secret Handbook (for Franchise and Distribution Companies). (ABA Publishing, 2000)

Lorinc, John. Opportunity Knocks: The Truth About Canada's Franchise Industry. (Prentice Hall, ISBN: 0134556933)

Mancuso, Joseph and Joseph R. Mancuso. Mancuso's Small Business Basics: Start, Buy or Franchise Your Way to a Successful Business. (Source Books Trade, 1997)

Matusky, Gregory. Best Home-Based Franchises. (Doubleday, 1992)

McDermott, Michael J. The Franchise Handbook, Winter 2000. (Enterprise Magazines, ISBN: 999888764X)

Meaney, James A. How To Buy A Franchise: An Experienced Franchise Lawyer Shows How To Find, Evaluate And Negotiate For the Right Franchise. (Greenport, NY: Pilot Books, 1999)

Mendelsohn, Martin. The Guide to Franchising. (International Publishing Group, 1999)

Mucciolo, Louis. Make It Yours: How to Own Your Own Business: Buy a Business, Start a Business, Franchise a Business. (John Wiley & Sons, ISBN: 0471625825)

Munna, Raymond J. Franchise Selection: Separating Fact from Fiction a Guide for Entrepreneurs, Investors, Attorneys, Accountants and Management Marketing Advisors. (Granite, 1988)

Nieman, Gideon. The Franchise Option: How to Franchise Your Business. (Juta & Co., 1998)

Patel, Jay. Franchising: Is It Fair? How to Negotiate an Equitable Franchise Agreement. (WeWrite Corp., 1999)

Perry, Robert Laurance. Fifty Best Low Investment, High-Profit Franchises. (Prentice Hall, 1990)

Powers, Mike. How to Open a Franchise Business: Reap the Benefits and Avoid the Pitfalls of Owning a Franchise. (William Morrow & Co, 1995)

Price, Stuart. The Franchise Paradox: New Directions, Different Strategies. (Continuum International Publishing, 1999)

PSI Research. The Franchise Bible. (PSI Research, 1994)

Purvin, Bobert L. Jr. The Franchise Fraud: How to Protect Yourself Before and After You Invest. (New York: John Wiley & Sons, 1994, Due also in December 2001)

Raab, Steve and Gregory Matusky. The Blueprint for Franchising a Business. (New York: John Wiley, 1987)

Raab, Steve. How to Buy a Franchise That's Right for You, 2 Audio Cassettes. (New York: John Wiley & Sons, ISBN: 0471629146)

Redden, Timothy T. Franchise Buyer's Handbook. (Addison-Wesley, 1989)

Rule, Roger C. The Franchise Redbook: Easy-To-Use Facts and Figures. (PSI Research, 1999)

Rule, Roger C. No Money Down Financing for Franchising. (Research Publishing Services, 1998)

Rust, Herbert. Owning Your Own Franchise. (Prentice Hall, 1991)

Scherer, Daniel J. Financial Security and Independence Through a Small Business Franchise. (Pilot Books, ISBN: 0875760023)

Services Industries Research Group. Retail and Franchise Market in China: A Strategic Entry Report, 2000. (Icon Group International, 2000)

Seid, Michael and Dave Thomas. Franchising for Dummies. (For Dummies, 2000)

Sherman, Andrew J. Franchising and Licensing: Two Ways to Build Your Business. New York: AMACOM, 1999)

Shivell, Kirk and Kent Shivell. The Franchise Kit. (New York: McGraw-Hill, 1995)

Shivell, Kirk and Kent B. Banning. Running a Successful Franchise. (New York: McGraw-Hill, ISBN: 0070569878)

Shook, Carrie and Robert L. Shook. Franchising: The Business Strategy That Changed the World. (Prentice Hall, 1993)

Shropshrire, Kenneth L. The Sports Franchise Game: Cities in Pursuit of Sports Franchises, Events, Stadiums, and Arenas. (University of Pennsylvania Press, 1995)

Spiegel, Robert. The Shoestring Entrepreneur's Guide to the Best Home-Based Franchises. (St. Martin's Press, 2000)

Spinelli, Stephen. Franchising: Pathway to Wealth Creation. (Financial Times Prentice Hall, 2003)

Stanworth, John and Brian Smith. The Barclays Guide to Franchising for the Small Business. (Blackwell Publishers, 1991)

Sterling Publishing Company. Franchise Opportunities: A Business of Your Own. (Sterling Publishing, 1995)

Stone, Phil. Buying a Franchise. (How to Books, 2001)

Thomas, Dave and Michael Seid. Franchising for Dummies. (Foster City, CA: IDG Books Worldwide, Inc., 2000)

Tomzack, Mary E. Tips & Traps When Buying a Franchise. (Oakland, CA: Source Book Publications, 1999)

Van Hoy, Jerry. Franchise Law Firms and the Transformation of Personal Legal Services. (Greenwood Publishing Group, 1997)

White, Philip D. and Mark R. Brackin. A Banker's Guide to Using Fee Income to Build Superior Profits and Long-Term Franchise Value. (Irwin Professional Publishing, 1998)

Whittemore, Meg, Andrew Sherman and Ripley Meg Hotch. Financing Your Franchise. (New York: McGraw-Hill, 1993)

Wilson, Jack. Nuts and Bolts of Buying a Business or Franchise. (CMN Press, 1998)

Wolfe, Rebecca Luhne, Rebecca R. Luhne and Nancy Shotwell. Buying Your First Franchise. (Crisp Publications, 1994)

Zaid, Frank. Canadian Franchise Guide. (Carswell Legal Publications, 2000)

Zwisler, Carl E. Master Franchising: Selecting, Negotiating and Operating a Master Franchise. (CCH, 1999)

Conclusion

Passive income is something most people only dream of. It is a fantasy, kind of like winning the lottery that will allow one to gain freedom from a 9 to 5 job and spend time doing the things they love.

But as you may already know from reading this eBook, passive income is no fantasy and is very different from winning the lottery. Winning the lottery is sheer luck, it is out of your hands and your chances of winning it are extremely slim.

Passive income on the other hand is something YOU control, it is entirely within your hands and something that can drastically change your life for the better.

Hmm, so what exactly am I trying to get at here?

Well, first of all YOU are responsible for setting yourself up with a monthly passive income. If you don't do the work, sit around and fantasize all day, you likely won't get a passive income that will give you a lot of financial freedom.

If you do get serious about this and do the work that is necessary to set up a reliable passive income... Well, if you do that you pretty much know what will happen: exactly what you are fantasizing about right now.

And to put the task ahead of you into perspective, it actually does NOT take a lot of work to set up your first income stream. It takes **concentrated work**.

If you currently work an 8 hour day 5 times a week, you spend somewhere around 160 hours a month making someone else rich.

If you can invest 25% of that time into setting up an income stream for yourself, fill that time with concentrated work and stick to your goal you can most probably have a passive income stream of $200 - $500 a month no problem.

So what I'm trying to say is: get to work, stick to it and don't get discouraged because passive income makes sense. Who knows, maybe in a few weeks you will have your phone bills, cable, gym, water and hydro bills taken care of every month – how far you take it from there will be entirely up to you!

www.ingramcontent.com/pod-product-compliance
Lightning Source LLC
Chambersburg PA
CBHW070328190526
45169CB00005B/1802